FRANCOIS!

*The Extraordinary Life &
Times of French Restauranteur
Francois Primpied*

John Maffin

Media Fizz Publishing

This book is for my late mother Eugenia Maffin whose dedication and love for family knew no bounds. Her Christian belief, work ethic, steely determination and selfless outlook shone a steady guiding light throughout my life. Mum was born in a village close to idyllic Lake Garda in Northern Italy. My father was a British soldier in WWII and they married at a church in Udine. After the war, she travelled alone by train and sea across a devastated European landscape to join my dad in Swanland. Mum's cooking skills were legendary – especially with her native Italian cuisine. A strong principled character, she passed away in 2015, aged 99 years with her mind and sense of humour intact.

John Maffin 2018

"Service is about delivering things that, as a customer, you didn't even know that you wanted...."

MICHELLE ROUX JNR

CONTENTS

INTRODUCTION

This is no run-of-the-mill biography about a restauranteur, his uncompromising service ethic and highly acclaimed cuisine. Rather, it is a unique, sometimes dramatic, often hilarious, occasionally reflective and always fascinating record of an incident-packed journey through a lifetime in the restaurant trade.

A friendly, colourful, gregarious and determined character, Jean Francois Pierre Primpied was born in the village of Bourg de Thizy near Roanne in the South-west of France. As an irrepressible eight-year-old, he played accordion on the same bill as international singing star Petula Clarke. His love of cooking and the business of serving good food was inspired by his grandmother who owned a village cafe. Later, through school years, this interest was developed in his mother's family kitchen. In his early teens, Francois was apprenticed at the Michelin three-star 'Les Freres Troigros' - at the time described as the world's best restaurant. As a passenger, he cheated death by a whisker in a horrific head-on car crash - aged just sixteen years.

For the purpose of advancement, the Troisgros family encouraged Francois develop his English language skills abroad. With their blessing he moved to Hull in East Yorkshire, England where he met Sue, his wife-to-be on, a dance floor. Unfashionable though the city was, he loved the people and work so much, he made his home in the area - and developed a cult-following in the hotels, restaurants and cafés where he worked – variously as employee, manager, director or owner. But for three years working in his own restaurant at Guines near Calais, he spent most of his working life in the restaurant trade in the East Riding of Yorkshire.

Over the years, Francois met and befriended internationally known personalities and A-list stars. He once drove the late French singing star Sacha Distel forty miles for a midnight meal of steak and chips. Even Del and Rodney Trotter were treated to a lift whilst they were filming ' Only Fools and Horses' in Hull. By chance, he shared a five hour train journey with Rolling Stones guitarist Bill Wyman. Whilst on holiday in Provence, he chatted with the group's singer Mick Jagger in a local shop. Later, he met John Thaw whilst shopping in a village market.

Francois was always an outgoing character who loved contact with people. He treated everyone with the same respect. Customers loved his food, his character - and his brand of fun. As much as on stage as a child, he was the ultimate showman in the front of house of any restaurant. In the kitchen, he was a hard taskmaster – but always fair, respectful and committed to developing individuals in his team. His life story charts the friendships that helped pull a needle of hope through the sometimes tightly woven fabric of opportunity - to eventually weave a golden pattern of success. The journey is a treasure-trove of anecdotes involving the rich and the famous - as well the friendly folk in East Yorkshire.

During his extensive career, Francois built a great reputation amongst diners and his contemporaries in the restaurant trade. However, he remained grounded and never lost touch with his core public - who always enjoyed exceptional food at reasonable cost. This fayre was always accompanied by a generous helping of banter, kindly humour and fine entertainment – with his beloved accordion often the instrument of choice.

A friend of all three professional sports clubs in Hull, his French credentials were utilised by Hull FC to clinch key transfers - and his sense of humour may well have affected the result of an England v France international match! Perhaps his funniest anecdote was an unexpected ad-hoc comedy routine in his Guines restaurant with Carmen Silvera who played Edith Melba Artois in the long-running British TV show 'Allo Allo.' In the same room, he played the accordion and on occasion served the then British Foreign Secretary Margaret Beckett - as she and her entourage made their way back home after summer caravan holidays abroad.

In a lifetime rooted in the art of preparing and serving great food, connections with people are what made Francois tick. For that reason, he spent most of his time at the front of house. He learned the meaning of hard work and realised an ambition to manage a top hotel. He also experienced the joys and stresses of running his own restaurant business. Above all, he entertained and was entertained by the public who were his customers and very often people he also saw as his friends.

This is his story.

EARLY YEARS

"I hate the ****ing French," stormed an incandescent Francois. Red faced, utterly frustrated and fuming with rage, the French-born restauranteur slammed down the telephone handset at the rear of his popular establishment at 159 Kingston Road Willerby in the East Riding of Yorkshire.

The outburst was completely out of character. He was known to be uncompromising with standards and firm in enforcing them, but a meltdown was not usually on the menu. Someone had just lit his blue touch paper and the now flaming rocket had fizzed skywards accompanied by a showering crackerjack of expletives. It was noon on a dull and breezy Thursday in late October 2010. Of course Francois is a patriot. He loves the country of his birth and its people. However, on the other end of the telephone line, had been an official of the French pension management organisation CNAVPL. The administrator's demeanour had seemed unhelpful, uncaring - and almost deliberately rigid. In his experience, it was characteristic of the way French government pen-pushers operated – seemingly with the intent to make sure the matter at hand was not cleared up anytime soon. It seemed to be a sort of job maintenance strategy. At least that is how it all felt to Francois. In perhaps the largest democratic bureaucracy on the planet, snail's pace was the standard speed of travel. And proud of it they were. The official had succeeded in turning a normally friendly, meticulously polite and totally reasonable fellow countryman into an erupting Vesuvius of frustration. The protracted international call had clearly not gone very well. It seemed that the calm-as-you-please bureaucrat had no intention, desire or perhaps even training to be of any assistance at all. In those respects, there was a global reputation to protect.

It had been clear that any hope of achieving clarity or brevity when it came to the provision of a simple answer to a simple question was but a pipe dream. From his own experiences and that of friends, it seemed to Francois that ob-fuscation, lethargy and bloody-mindedness were common characteristics of French government departments. It was not something he was pre-pared to tolerate. Already as high as a kite, hav-ing been queued on the international call for a long period, the experience had been utterly insufferable. He was angry. In the restaurant, as ever, many jobs needed attention. Business was steady despite the recession, but the rewards for unceasing hard work were relatively modest. Chancellor of the Exchequer George Osborne's aus-terity had started and was affecting the confidence and mindset of clients who were already eating-out less frequently. Ordering fresh produce from local suppliers at prices that could make the menu affordable was ever a priority. Turnover was one thing, but the bottom-line quite another – especially when there was to be no compromise on the quality of ingredients. The long-lasting shine from running his own business was increasingly becoming tarnished by the long hours and rising costs in a tight and stuttering financial climate. Through his long career in catering, both in France and subsequently in the East Riding of Yorkshire, it had all been largely a pleasure. Francois loved engaging with customers and pleasing them with his food and service. Banter was his drug of choice in the daily struggle to earn a living and keep fatigue at bay. The days were long and the pressure unceasing. However, now in his 60's and feeling more and more tired, questions about what should come next were nagging. Was it now time for a change? In fact, for one reason or another, the question had cropped up several times before.

Although it was outside normal opening hours, a passing client and friend had spotted Francois silhouetted at the back of the restaurant. Entering the darkened premises through the unlocked front door in the final seconds of the call, the visitor saw the funny side of the outburst. "That's made my day," grinned the retired gentleman as he slalomed stylishly between the tables, which some customers found just a little too close to each other on busy nights. Taken a little by surprise, Francois composed himself quickly and within a few moments, on the outside at least, had resumed his usual friendly and calm demeanour. As a diabetic, he knew that too much stress caused an increase in adrenaline and could trigger other chemical imbalances leading to dangerous blood-sugar levels. Was it a plot by the French authorities to save money by finishing him off early, he mused? Confiding in the still chuckling visitor Francois shared the details of another bad experience with the authorities just after he'd first arrived in England. On that occasion, it had been Her Majesty's Revenue and Customs that had wound him up. Christened 'Jean-Francois' Pierre Primpied, the hyphened forenames translated as the English surname 'John' and French man.'

On arrival in Hull in his late teens to work at the Royal Station Hotel, the UK taxman had assumed a fundamentally flawed position on his gender – addressing correspondence to Miss Jean-Francois Primpied. In the UK, Jean is universally assumed to be a female name whilst in France it is malev - derived from the old French Jehan. For Jean-Francois, it was the first and final straw on the subject. To avoid any further confusion, he immediately elected to be known simply as "Francois." In all the years since, including a three-year return to the country of his birth, Francois firmly remained an Anglophile. His love of cooking and his desire to spend a lifetime in the business of creating and serving fine food was inspired by childhood family influences.

In June 1952, England-based Jaroslav Drobny won his second straight men's tennis title beating Australia's Frank Sedgeman in the French Championships. In the same competition, it was America's Doris Hart that took the women's crown. In that same month, Freddie Trueman made his England cricket debut and Elizabeth II became Queen of England and the United Kingdom. Meanwhile, in Bourg-de-Thizy, 74 kilometres north-west of Lyon, close to Roanne in the Rhone-alps region of eastern France another significant event took place. In the Primpied household, the birth of Jean-Francois Pierre trumped all other announcements. In the old days, it was French custom to use a godfather's forename as a middle name. Brother Pierre was ten years his senior. Father, Leon, was a local cabinet maker, whilst his mother Juliette worked full-time as a machinist in a local factory. In making family garments at home to save money, her skills were turned to good effect. Family finances were further improved by selling what she had made in what became a tiny cottage industry. Already hard-working in her employment and running the home, it was a case of needs-must - and a testimony to her dedication, work ethic and determined character.

Juliette Primpied

Despite all the other pressures, she still found the time to prepare family meals at least twice a day – coming home in her lunch break to perform the mid-day ritual. It was an arduous life in post-war times, but the country was now at peace. People were friendly and resolute in making the best of what little they had. Until his death when Francois was just five, papa provided much-needed income and support to sustain the family's large, rented house. His passing was a traumatic event and an emotional blow to the family. The tragic loss also placed them under significantly increased financial pressure. Yet, those were not the days of raised expectations and plenty. Rather, what prevailed was a post-war rural economy where 'grow your own' was not a fashion or health fad. It was an imperative. Make do and mend was the order of the day. The family vegetable garden was cultivated with enthusiasm, care and respect - for upon the fruits of their labour, survival depended. Looking back, Francois recalls his childhood and the circumstances and reality of their situation.

"It was simple really. We had little money and I learned the value of the garden and the benefits of fresh, healthy food. It was very much a way of life away from the big cities. We had that survival instinct. There was little choice in the matter. We grew all types of vegetables and fruits. I loved the smell and taste of strawberries and ate many as I picked! The meat that we cooked came from the chickens and rabbits we raised ourselves. In this way, we learned about humility and the way to survive on a tiny budget. Of course, there were times when we had to buy things from the village shops, but in general we lived a basic life without luxuries. As a kid, I used to fish a lot. My uncle was a bank manager in Cambrai in Northern France. He was a very-kind man and used to come and see us and stay for up to three weeks at a time. He was married to my mother's sister. On three or four days in a week, we would go fishing together at the nearby river from seven o' clock in the morning. I loved my uncle. He got to his retirement and was hoping to spend time relaxing. Having retired at the end of one week, the following Wednesday, they held a big retirement dinner for him with many guests. As he got out of the car, he collapsed and died of a heart attack. It was a massive shock to us."

Francois has vivid memories of his childhood days. His recollections shine a light on the the simple foods and scant means at his family's disposal. Bourg-de-Thizy had a small population of some 2,300 people. Surrounded by hills, meadows and rolling countryside its community was closely connected, not only with the farming fraternity, but with the business of local factory production on the outskirts of the town. The centre flourished with a myriad of essential shops and small café establishments. It was a close-knit community with a strong commitment to religious worship. This was borne out by the various churches that have been constructed in the area over many centuries. The cobbled central square was dominated by the impressive architecture of Eglise Saint-Pierre (St Peter's Church).

Situated on the opposite side of the street to the main entrance door of the church were quaint three-story buildings, some having ground floor commercial use. Grandma's cafe (Cafe du Midi) was a smaller and adjacent two-story building. In later years, the street was given a significant face-lift with some demolition of houses which were located to the left of the image below to give a town square feature alongside the church. This facilitated easy parking and gave the area a modern feel. Visitors to the church and events held there would augment the local footfall and help keep the kitchen busy - especially on weekends when services and wedding ceremonies would be held. Regardless of the changes in recent years, Bourg-le-Thizy retains the close-knot community feel of days past - although it has now merged in name with nearby communes to become Thizy-les-Bourgs.

Old image showing the premises which would become Cafe du Midi - the building immediately below the couple pictured farthest away. The street was eventually given a makeover and a wider square developed.

Grandma's industry and cooking skills were an inspiration for Francois who dreamed from her example, that one day he too would run his own restaurant business. Although post-war austerity caused many to live a fairly basic lifestyle, France is historically associated with life's finer things – including gastronomy, fashion, perfumery and wines. The latter is integral to French culture. Almost every region in France is involved with wine production. With vast areas of land devoted to viniculture, the quality produced is widely acknowledged to be the best in the world. Equally, French food has a global reputation - and these influences were well focused upon a young Francois as he saw at first-hand how country folk enjoyed their little luxuries.

"As a child, I would spend quite a lot of time in my grandma's Café du Midi. It was fascinating for me. There was a cellar and I remember wandering in there amongst the barrels. The wine was decanted every morning from the 100-litre kegs into pots to be drunk by customers in the café. At first, the aroma seemed a little strange and I associated it with adults. I had no desire to taste it myself. France is full of wine lovers and it is a fundamental part of the way of life. As children reach their teens, they may try sips, but generally I would say it is much later in life before they might drink it routinely. Although it is legal to drink wine at younger ages, there is a minimum age to be able to buy it in the shops. Kids would go into a café with their parents and get a free 'grenadine' drink. It was loved by all children in France."Interestingly, the word 'grenadine' is derived from the French word 'grenade' – translated as 'pomegranate' in English. "

The original formulation was pomegranate juice, water and sugar. However, when sold commercially, some manufacturers have replaced the fruit with artificial ingredients. The product is sold all over the world and used as an ingredient in cocktails. Café du Midi (Coffee of the South) was a simple working-class establishment with planked wooden floors, and natural wood fittings including counters, tables and chairs. It was in this rustic haven that up to twenty locals gathered regularly for lunch and a chat. Given the small size of the establishment, this represented full to busting! To them, this was important way of satisfying their human instinct for socialisation. There were no bowling alleys, multi-screen theatres or theme parks at hand. Such facilities were decades away in the future and reserved for larger communities. Using the French equivalent of the English "slate" grandma noted the spending of villagers in a little book and payment always made at the end of the week. In the café, there was an overflow room on the first floor which was used for holding events. As the memories flooded back, Francois recalled:

"In the evenings, local people would gather to have a natter, eat food, drink wine and play cards. It wasn't an expensive place and it provided somewhere for people to mix and relax after a hard day at work. Town folk wanted to meet with friends and neighbours - rather than always be confined to their own houses. In those days, television was a rarity and almost non-existent in rural villages. Distractions other than domestic chores, were few and far between. People were friendly to each other and everyone knew everyone else. It was a close-knit community. I remember that each evening Monsieur Fayot, a local farmer, would come to the restaurant with a large container of fresh and still-warm milk. People would then buy this product, according to what they needed and then take it home in their own pots. The café was a popular meeting place and stayed open until around 9pm. At weekends, when the church held services and events like weddings or funerals, people would come to eat and drink together. The café, the community and the institutions were integrated closely into the normal lives of people. In the village, we had a pharmacy, three butchers, three bakers and nine little bars – one of which also served petrol. I sometimes wondered whether the phrase 'getting tanked up" came from such a place where fuel and wine could be obtained under the same roof! In the old times in France, the words café and 'bar' described similar places. The tradition was for the some of the men to call off at a café on the way to work. This would be from 6.30am. Some of the menfolk would have a small coffee with a touch of brandy. Others might drink a small glass of wine and have a chat. These beverages would occasionally be taken with bread or croissants purchased from the local bakery. Alcohol was never far away from French lips on an average day.

"About mid-morning the local farmers, who in summer would have started work at 5am, would arrive at the cafés and drink pots of red or white wine. They would bring their own bread, sandwiches, garlic sausages, goat's cheese, pork scratchings or whatever – all purchased from the local shops. They would drink sensibly and have their break, talking to local friends from different farms. It was a way of ensuring that they did not become depressed by being isolated in the countryside. From 11.30, on their way home for their lunch hour, some of the factory workers would pop-in to the café - again for a quick aperitif. Having eaten at home, they might also meet again for a little tipple whilst waiting for the same factory bus which had dropped them off earlier. In hard times, little pleasures meant a lot. In those days, the afternoon shifts were normally worked between 2pm and 6pm. When the factory bus dropped them off in the village at the end of the day, some workers might call off yet again at the café for a quick drink. Others would stay for a longer drinking session and go home a bit jolly! Food at home would be normally prepared and ready for no later than 8.30pm. People could eat in the cafes up until a similar time. On weekdays, they went to bed early, but at the weekend they would stay up later and enjoy eating out – sometimes until the early hours. For the French, dining-out is part of a way of life which embraces long conversations - often stretching across an entire evening."

Francois' school years comprised of attending a nursery for a year from age four. It was conveniently located next door to the family home. The hours were from 8-11.30am and again in the afternoon from 2 to 6pm. The arrangement perfectly fitted with mum's working hours at the local factory. From five years of age, he attended a boys' school in the centre of the village. It was just a four-minute walk away. At age twelve, the family received a grant for Francois so that he could attend a live-in school in Roanne. Over the next couple of years, whilst he performed to a mediocre standard at best academically, his talents at the billard table came on leaps and bounds. As a kid he'd spend hours in the bar La Terrase in Bourg-le-Thizy honing the skills. Selected as a young teen to take part in the French Billiards Championships, he was beaten only in the semi-finals.

"I was a bit of a rebel at the school and showed no academic interest whatsoever. I loved sport and did well at basketball and loved watching sport on a television set that we had eventually managed to buy. As a family we were still relatively poor and although I could have stayed-on for a couple of years more, I decided to leave and get work."

A poor outcome from all the years of compulsory schooling was somewhat predictable. Possibly, this was a result of his perception of restricted life chances and a lack of confidence at the outset that he could raise his sights above the limited prospects that were available in the immediate locality. He was living in difficult times and enjoying the moment was the order of the day. This feeling of hopelessness, leading to a present-time orientation seems to transcend time and peoples. In modern days faced with these frustrations, youngsters can easily drift into unhealthy dependencies upon drink or drugs – leading to criminal behaviour. There are alternatives and much can depend on upbringing, circle of friends and general support - as well as the ability and determination of an individual person to rise above the pressures and temptations that appear. Francois had no such distractions or desire to stray from a path that was straight and narrow. When he was just five years old, his elder brother Pierre followed in his father's footsteps and joined with a few of his friends to form a band. Practice sessions were conducted in the uppermost floor of the family house. The accordion, a quintessential French icon, lent a lively melody to the band's sound - albeit with notes of underlying melancholy.

Brother Pierre on stage

Although, the property was spacious, its fur-
nishings and floorcoverings were simple and in-
expensive. The architecture of local dwellings was
characterised by dingy cement-rendered exteriors,
shallow pitched roofs and shuttered windows.
Properties in the centre of town were up to four
stories high. It was a scene typical of many small
French villages and communes in the immediate
post-war era. Thankfully, they had largely escaped
the ravages of war which had damaged the hous-
ing stock of larger towns and cities. However, it
would be over a period of decades before the national economy would recover to the point where
smaller town businesses would find their feet and
local authorities could look to improve the public
domain. Francois was happy enough and just got

on with life, making the best of things.

The Primpied family home in Bourg-de-Thizy with mother Yvette pictured

The house was of such a large size that it was occasionally used as a venue for invited locals to arrive and dance to the music. The sounds from these events inspired Francois and fired his ambition to perform on stage. Although he was banned from the music practice room, one day his curiosity and enthusiasm got the better of him. Finding the room key by chance, he sneaked up the creaking stairs and stood nervously in front of the forbidden door. He allowed himself to dismiss from his mind the real threat of serious trouble should he be discovered. The key turned easily in the lock, but momentarily he felt a sense of tingling unease as he turned the creaking door handle. As he closed the door behind himself, his eyes feasted on the instruments set out in the room. In turn, he picked them up, imagining that he was the artist on stage. Within minutes, throwing caution to the wind, he was wildly banging out rhythms on the drum kit. The sensation of making sounds was intoxicating. Drawn to the transfer of emotion into the instrument, pent-up frustrations found a voice, if not yet an audience. Rather than the transgression being a one-off event, entering the room became a regular piece of mischief - whenever he was alone in the house. Almost inevitably, his naughtiness would eventually be discovered. One day, brother Pierre arrived home unexpectedly and heard enthusiastic, but still primitive, drumbeats emanating from the music room.

"My brother came into the room without warning. Probably, he'd first heard the racket in the street outside. He told me that he had listened for a while in the corridor. I was expecting to be told off because I should not have been in there. Surprisingly, he wasn't angry at all. In fact, he encouraged me to learn to play properly! He asked me to the next rehearsal of his band - and promised to give me lessons. He even bought me a small accordion and taught me to play that instrument as well. I was really over the moon to be taken seriously and encouraged. Soon after, I played my first gig as drummer with the band! It was in front of several hundred people and we finished the session at 2am. Talk about being thrown in at the deep end!"

Still a small child, Francois was stepping outside the normal experiences of a primary schoolboy. The close association with his elder brother and the band bred a high degree of self-confidence and helped develop his natural outgoing spirit and sense of fun. Late nights became the norm. The genie was out of the bottle! Although the little French kid was being given some slack, he was still in a protective bubble overseen by his mum and brother. It was a balancing act for them - and their aim was to try and keep him safe and as grounded as possible. By the time he'd reached seven years old, mum came to the view that it was time to bring her hyperactive son to heel. At times finding it difficult to control her youngest, she hatched a plot to expose him to a regime of tight discipline and hard work. Francois has a vivid recollection of his temporary summer banishment to the countryside:

"At that time, you could say that I was a little prat. Mum struggled to control me. I was always out playing boules and getting into mischief. We had a relative who owned a farm - so I was sent there to experience the country life. I knew it would be a problem. It just wasn't for me. When I arrived, I found that there were about six other kids there. They were excited to be on the farm. I was devastated! We were surrounded by clucking chickens, mooing cows and barking dogs. The living conditions could best be described as basic. We were expected to help milking the cows and do other jobs around the place. All of the kids were expected to sleep in the barn. We had little beds and were expected to turn-in at 7pm so that we could get up at 5am. It was impossible. I was a night person and never went to sleep until extremely late. By using a torch, I stayed awake on the first night and read 'Micky Parade' - a children's comic. It wasn't long before I became extremely fed-up. One of the girls was of a similar mind. The next night, we found the light switch and turned it on. Unfortunately, the farmer saw what we'd done and to fix our little game, he turned-off the main switch at the barn's fuse board. Once he'd gone, we located the main fuses and threw the switch back on again. Our luck ran out though, because the farmer's wife saw the lights and put two and two together. She stormed in and told me off. That should have been that, but the girl decided to defy the woman and put the lights back on. Unfortunately, she blew some fuses at the farmhouse in the process and we were both sent home the next morning. She was upset and blamed me for being a bad influence! I was over the moon to be getting out of the place. When I appeared back home after just two days away, my mum and brother were not best pleased."

Aged 8 years and with his nascent musical talent rapidly evolving, Francois and brother Pierre found themselves playing accordion with another band who called themselves "Rhythm and Blues." Their biggest night came when they played as a supporting act for emerging female British talent – Petula Clark who was touring France. Eventually, she would become an International star of stage, screen and radio. Following her 1957 appearance at the Paris Olympia 'Pet' Clark signed with the Vogue record label and collaborated with Claud Wolff – the man who would become her future husband. After her 1960 French tour with international singing star Sacha Distel, who remained a close friend until his death in 2004, she recorded "Sailor" which became a number one hit in the UK. Her career then blossomed. Eventually she became the first person to be subject of the TV programme 'This is Your Life' on three occasions. Other hits included 'Downtown' penned by Tony Hatch and 'This is My Song.' Francois vividly recalls the night in front of around 2000 people when he was on stage as her supporting act in his home-town Bourg De Thizy:

"At the time, Pet Clark was a well-known performer in the UK and France – but not yet quite the international superstar she would later become. Along with another band above us in the pecking order, we were her supporting act. I remember playing on stage and seeing her standing in the wings watching us. I was just a small boy. We came off to loud applause. It was intoxicated with the occasion. As I walked off-stage towards her, she was smiling broadly. As I reached her, she ruffled my hair and told me I had been "very good." She spoke French very well. It is a great memory."

The band then played regularly in places across the region. Approaching teen years, Francois recalls they were then booked under the title 'The Primpied Brothers,' even though only he and Pierre were family members. With a singer fronting the act, their sound included guitar, accordion, drums, trumpet, sax and bass. It was a big sound, in any language. Things did not always go well at gigs. Audiences were always entertained and ever appreciative. However, on one occasion disorder broke out on the dance floor. In a matter of just a few minutes, the fighting had escalated to a point where police had to be called to take control. Just prior to the arrival of the gendarmes, things took a significant turn for the worse as violence spilled on to the stage. This escalation was clearly becoming dangerous - especially for the artists. Should they play the national anthem - or run for it? Francois was a little helpless, being armed only with drumsticks - and well out of his depth in terms of physicality. His brother had an extremely expensive accordion to protect and necessarily avoided getting directly involved in the warfare. Fortunately, Pierre the guitarist was a member of the Compagnies Republicaines de Sécurité – better known as the CRS – the French national riot police. He was certainly worth his weight in gold when it came to protecting his mates on stage. Francois has a vivid recollection of what happened next:

"Pierre set about the attackers with his guitar. He was swinging it round and each time it connected with one of them a piece flew off. It was like a performance of The Who – but with the guitar being smashed over the wildly disorderly audience rather than the stage! His drastic actions had the effect of calming down the offenders - just prior to the arrival of police. The scene resembled the aftermath of a saloon brawl in a wild west cowboy movie!"

Whilst was not clear why the fisticuffs had commenced, the presence of alcohol is often the catalyst for confrontation. Yet, when Nutella cut their prices by 70% in 2018, French supermarket aisles became a war zone with brawling customers throwing punches, pulling hair and shoving elderly shoppers aside. Le Parisien reported that such disgreeable events were rare and more typical of developing countries where there is a shortage of essential products.

In 2020, a semi-professional rugby match between Tarbes and Lannemezan resulted in victory for the home team by a score of 36-3. However, the match was described in the media as a red-blooded collison of the two sides during which seven red cards were shown - five of which were issued in the early stages when the violence drew in the management and resulted in a seven-minute stoppage.

Where is there a guitarist when you need one?

Class of 1959/60: Francois 2nd pupil from the right - middle row

Although Francois did not particularly enjoy what he felt was the hum-drum element of school days, he does have some happy memories. He attended a quite small school with a limited number of teachers. Prominent amongst them was a kindly headmaster who also doubled as a form teacher. He was held in high esteem by all his pupils. Each year, the children would show their appreciation by holding a surprise party during which presents would be given and a good time had by all. The party day was always kept a secret from the teacher. In the year that the event was organised by Francois, he contributed with music on the accordion accompanied by a fellow pupil who sang a song. This attachment with school days persisted into adulthood. Each year, the menfolk of the village held an event to celebrate the passing of a decade since their school days. Termed 'Fetes des Classe' [class parties] the ten-year cohort would meet former classmates in celebration of the tenth anniversary of their leaving. The occasion, which was held on a Sunday, included a procession through the streets led by majorettes. Francois has vivid memories of seeing the events both as a child and in later years as an adult participant with his schooldays cohort.

"As a kid, I remember one of the several bands playing, 'When the Saints Go Marching In.' Each ten-year group would dress in a style which reflected their age. The first age group was the twenty year- olds and they would be dressed smartly, but in the modern style. Each lead row would display a banner depicting the group's age. As people got older, their dress would be more and more conventional. Those who had mobility problems would be conveyed in vintage cars. I missed my fifty and sixty-year events but recall one year where the forty-year olds were dressed up as cartoon characters. After the morning procession, participants would go to the war memorial to pay respects to those of our friends of who had been lost in the war.

"The priest said prayers and the national anthem 'La Marseilles' was played. It was very moving. Celebrations continued into the evening and overnight through to the following day. After a celebratory meal, family and friends were welcome to attend a firework display where youngsters would dance around a fire singing. A brass brand entertained the crowd playing old fashioned tunes. Cafés stayed open and were always busy. At around 9.30 pm, those who were old enough went to the City Hall for dancing until five or six in the morning. It was for those who had the stamina. Each age group would socialise with their contemporaries."

Whilst there may be variations from school to school and also regional differences, the reunions do seem to be popular and well-supported local events where they do take place. Although Francois was not able to attend every Fetes des Classe, it was something that he enjoyed.

Like many contemporaries, he would happily make a long round-trip to partipate. To the outsider, it may seem like a case of any excuse for a party followed by a serious pilgramage to the wine caves, but there is also a genuine spirit of community and nostalgia for school days. Little wonder given the 24-hour school week, one and a half to two-hour lunch breaks and lack of insistence on uniform.

Francois far-right at one of the Fetes des Classe ten-year celebrations

So embedded was this event in the local community, that local employers allowed the ten-year (dix-ans) groups time-off on the following day to attend trips to visit the wine caves in the Beaujolais region – about an hour's drive away by coach.

"A coach was available outside the town hall for those that wanted to continue the celebrations. The Monday itinerary included wine tasting and visits to local cheese farms. It would all come to a finish about 8pm on the Monday so that there was time to sober up for work on the following day!"

In his childhood, Francois saw that families were never far from poverty. The food basics were to a great extent in their own hands through garden cultivation. Home living comforts were barely more than primitive for that age and aside from social gatherings and sporting endeavours in the village, entertainment was based on simple technologies such as radio. The nature of the family unit has changed over the years, but they grew from those closely-knit extended families, that pooled resources for the common good.

"Although people were poor by today's standards, they were happy enough. The older folk had come through two world wars that had ravaged Europe. Children knew nothing about those dark days, but for their parents it was a relief to be living in peace. Various friendly forms of entertainment in the village were available at weekends - and included boules or petanque. There were discos and cycle races. Once or twice a year a small fair would arrive in the square with rides and shooting galleries. This was extremely exciting for the kids."

But times were changing and the appearance of industrial enterprises close-by did offer some opportunities for more people to raise their living standards. A significant local development was the Treca factory. The company was founded in 1935 by Rene Moritz. He was a prominent chemical engineer who had visionary ideas about developing what at the time was an almost non-existent bedding market. His idea was to use high resistance springs in mattresses with a wool fabric. It was a quantum leap forward from straw pallets used hitherto and revolutionised the bedding market.

The company became the flagship of French industry.

"Treca were the big local factory employers. My brother Pierre had his first job in their factory. They produced textiles and matrasses. There were a lot of farmers in the area who produced butter and cheese. Monsieur and Madame Longere also had a small factory in the village. The ability to have work and to be able to eat and enjoy seeing their children grow-up was something to be thankful for - and there was always hope for a better future."

Traditionally, the family plays a central role in French culture. Greetings are often through kissing on the cheek in all adult interactions – except man to man, where handshakes are more common. With strangers, it is deemed polite to be formal and maintain reservation with quiet tones generally deemed to be the norm. Food is routinely made with great care and enthusiasm, with meals an opportunity for socialising with others. French cooking is known throughout the world, but regional variations exist. Seafood and cheeses have prominence on the Normandy region, whereas there is an emphasis on beef in Burgundy. Whilst traditional French cuisine can be characterised by its sauces, cheeses and breads, there has been a general shift away from complicated dishes characterised by heavy sauces. Although Bourg de Thizy was just a small village, its population needed access to basic services. There was little crime in the area - but police were available to investigate and deter offences. A fire brigade contingent covered three neighbouring villages. The new generation of children were now running through the streets. Their hopes and futures were pinned on a lasting peace and the emergence of new opportunities. Whilst some would remain in the local village, for many the new horizons were only to be seen further afield.

FINDING EXCELLENCE

With no real interest in academic achievement, a slim, dark-haired Francois left school at age thirteen - as was quite the norm in France at the time. Job opportunities in his home town remained severely limited. In any case, he had no clear idea about what career to follow. Although he had considered becoming a hairdresser, following in the footsteps of his cousin, becoming a chef or restauranteur had greater appeal - not least because of childhood influences in grandma's café.

Performances on-stage had also introduced a taste for acclaim. Becoming a chef, in a country noted for its fine cuisine offered the possibility of recognition and perhaps the possibility of fame. In France, catering in those days was viewed as being a solid and worthwhile career. Initially, Francois found low-paid employment at Le Relais de la Diligence in the nearby village of Lentilly. It was a useful introduction to the catering trade. He began working for a boss who had a kind demeanour and a thoughtful and caring approach toward his workers. The boss also had a second restaurant in the provincial capital city of Lyon - about half an hour away by car. Chez Joseph in Lyon was to be found in fashionable Rue Tupin. The city district was a sliver of narrow streets with buildings typically five or six floors high. Bordered by rivers along its length, access to the wider city was made possible by a multitude of bridges on either side. The area was awash with restaurants, pavement cafes and stylish shops. Tourists would stroll casually at peace with the world, whilst locals bustled about their business, more fixated on their daily imperatives. Francois recalls the times when he was asked to cover at the Lyon restaurant:

"Although I was resident in the Lentilly restaurant, where rooms were also available for customers, the boss would take some of us to help at the Lyon establishment to cover for holiday or sickness. He was a very nice man. We'd go with him about four in the afternoon. Knowing that we had a long shift ahead of us, he would kindly buy us something to eat on the way. We'd travel back at about one or two in the morning."

For Francois, this was a great example of how employees should be treated. They felt part of a team and were shown genuine respect. It was hard work, but that was how the trade operated. Another great lesson, which would become a feature of his own style later in his career, was the value of entertainment as part of the dining experience. In addition to his excellent cooking skills, the owner would appear in the restaurant later in the evenings and talk to clients. He would tell jokes and play the accordion. Although the tables were close to each other, people would get up and dance in the aisles. Francois liked this because he already had experience playing on the stage. He was as keen as mustard to develop his skills in the restaurant business. In Bourg de Thizzy, just a few doors from home, was a butcher's shop. The kindly proprietor was only too happy to give the teen a chance to learn about how to cut meat. More than that, it was agreed that he'd become involved in learning about all aspects of the trade. In those days, in the rural areas, butchers fed their own animals in preparation for slaughter. The shopkeeper was no exception and retained several cows in a field just outside the village. When the day came to transport a couple of them to the local abattoir, an excited Francois was only too pleased to jump on board the Citroen van.

The aim was to coax a couple of the cows into the back of the vehicle. It was to be a quite tight fit and not the easiest of tasks - even for a seasoned hand. For an inexperienced youngster it was a daunting prospect. The process involved using a degree of muscle and strength, both of which he lacked. In the event, it was the cow that not only won the almighty heave-ho, but also managed to triumphantly ease the panting Francois into a copious pile of dung. With the lad skidding around helplessly in the vile muck, the grown-ups could barely control their mirth. Such was the strength of odour and the volume of excrement, that the young Francois had to immediately make off home on foot for a wash and change of clothing. On arrival at the house, his mum was so alarmed at the stench and the splattered trail of bovine poop around the house that she felt compelled to give her son a crisply delivered swipe round the ears. His have-a-go attitude had been respected by the farmer, but unsurprisingly this impression was not immediately recognised back at home. Having scraped the offending material from his person, a washed and changed Francois now headed towards the abattoir for round two. The waiting butcher found himself once more impressed by the lad's determination. Whilst a detailed description of operations in slaughterhose is avoided, those who feel a great deal of sympathy for the unfortunate animal will take some consolation from the unfolding events:

"I arrived at the abattoir, washed and changed. Fresh as a daisy, I had no idea what to expect, but as a teenager I seemed that I was being treated as an adult. I felt as if I was a boy turning into a man. I wasn't squeamish or anything like that - even though slaughtering an animal isn't a pleasant process by any means. Unfortunately for me, as we prepared ourselves, the animal again unloaded a large amount of excrement on to the floor and I slipped right into the morass of dung. I was covered in the stuff and had to leave immediately and go back home to wash and change once again.

For the second time that day my mum clipped me round the ears for trailing the dung into the house. I can say that I was, without any shadow of doubt, well and truly in the shit that day!"

As a teenager, Francois was intrigued by the possibility of utilising transport other than his own legs. He dreamed of owning some wheels. With this prospect in mind, one day he spied a motorised bicycle for sale which he felt would fall within his borrowing remit - and admirably suit his purposes. The 49cc VolosoleX had an engine mounted just above the front forks. It was conceived during WWII by French manufacturer Solex who were owned variously by Dassault, Renault and Motobecane/MBK with more than 7 million units being sold globally prior to the cessation of production in France in 1988.

Afterwards, it was manufactured under licence in China and Hungary before returning to French manufacture in 2005 - with the latest electric model being foldable. As a matter of fact and as the reader will soon learn, the bike's versatility to assume a less rigid shape was by chance discovered some years earlier - by Francois! Looking back, it is hard to imagine that such a mode of transport would attract ownership by a French teen with an eye for skirt and a plan to impress. Yet, Italian author Primo Levi in his short stories collection 'The Periodic Table' wrote that he would be able to upgrade from bicycle to VeloSoleX in the event of a deal being successfully completed with a cosmetics company. So, perhaps being seen riding a motorised bicycle could be quite fashionable - and something of a success symbol?

Other celebrities adopted a 'needs must' approach to the machine. Rowan Atkinson in the 2007 Mr Bean film "Hitchhiker" found that his own bicycle had been flattened by a passing tank. Stranded in the French countryside, he begins thumbing a lift. In the distance, he sees an approaching VeloSoleX. Frustrated at its extremely slow progress towards him, he lies down for a comedic nap. In due course, the motorised bike arrives. It is being ridden by a large, scruffy old man who helpfully offers Bean a lift on the rear parcel rack. Unfortunately, now laden down, the machine fails to move. Exploiting the owner's momentary dismount, Bean hijack's the machine and fully opens the throttle. As he moves off, the machine's woeful lack of speed is lampooned by the film as a side shot of Bean attempting a getaway reveals the slowly plodding owner coming into view alongside – to snatch-back the snail's pace moped. Judging by the film, a speedometer would have been of little use – with an egg-timer or calendar more than sufficient to track progress!

In fairness, flat-out, the VeloSoleX could reach a heady speed of some 16 mph. The machine was not cheap. In fact, its second-hand purchase price was equivalent to around five month's pay for a young lad working at Le Relais de Diligence. Unfortunately, in lending Francois the cash, his generous restaurant boss failed to exercise any diligence at all. Despite weekly repayments stretching into adulthood, Francois was nevertheless delighted at last to be the owner of his own motorised transport. Using the machine for work made every good sense. However, saving the precious fuel to impress the girls on a weekend seemed a better choice at the time. And so, it was on a summer Sunday that he embarked on a local spin to win the heart of a local teens. The bike was no hand-built Noigier and he was not quite Jean-Francois Balde. However, he was a determined trier:

"I had big hopes for the bike. One weekend, I decided to ride it up the side of a very steep slope on the edge of town. On the way down a track, I saw some girls that I knew. They shouted and smiled at me. I was struggling with the speed downhill and the brakes were not the best. Unfortunately, I got distracted by the girls, lost control completely, hit a tree and wrote the bike off. I still had to pay off the loan which was a real pain."

This was not the first or indeed the most serious collision he would suffer. The next one, as a faultless passenger in a car on a public road demonstrated graphically that inexperienced and foolhardy driving could have much more serious and even fatal consequences. As part of his career progression, at the age of sixteen years, Francois attended vocational training at a local catering college. He found the course interesting and a sound formal basis for a future in the industry. At the end of those studies, it was necessary to complete final examinations. It was on the journey to undertake those important assessments that Francois and two fellow students were involved in a catastrophic car crash. Sitting in the front passenger seat, Francois was helpless as the driver sped towards a bend and entered a reckless blind overtaking manoeuvre into an horrific head-on collision with a fast sports car travelling in the opposite direction. The smash resulted in the small Citroen 2CV car being forced under the lorry it was seeking to overtake. Tragically, the female driver died instantly. Immediately losing consciousness at the time of impact and after two weeks in coma, the only fleeting recollection of the incident for Francois was the words of firemen discussing the importance of cutting him free from the wreckage.

He was taken to hospital with two shattered knees, and a broken left shoulder. In the six agonising months that followed, he underwent six operations and was left with scars which decades later acted as reminders of the tragedy. To progress, Francois' decided that the time was ripe to look for a new job. Given the lack of suitable local opportunities, he was left with no option but to seek employment further afield – as many others from the village had done before him. On the recommendation of Zaza, an old headwaiter who lived in the village, Francois applied for an apprenticeship at Les Freres Troisgros - a restaurant in Roanne - some twenty-five kilometres away. Whilst he understood that the establishment had an excellent reputation, he had not quite comprehended the magnitude of opportunity that was about to unfold.

* * *

The Troisgros restaurant dynasty had begun with Jean-Baptiste and Marie (Badaut) Troisgros. They owned Hotel Moderne in Roanne, close to Lyon. Their sons Pierre and Jean developed their culinary talents with Fernand Point at La Pyramide in Vienne. Contemporaries included Paul Bocuse - who became their lifelong friend. Whilst Point was a strict and hard taskmaster, he and his apprentice Bocuse were known to be prolific pranksters upon unsuspecting visitors - especially well-heeled Parisian tourists who were lured to sit in the kitchen to taste a complimentary delicacy. Meanwhile, hidden under the table, Bocuse white-washed their heels. When one day a local gendarme arrived, he was distracted by Point long enough for Bocuse to paint the officer's cycle a bright pink colour. In due course, taking charge of their parent's restaurant, the Troisgros brothers transformed it into a distinguished gastronomic destination which embraced the revolutionary nouvelle cuisine. Although the style was influenced by the austerity of Japanese cooking, with tiny portions on large white plates, this was never countenanced by Pierre and Jean. Instead, they brought to the fore the virtues of seasonal ingredients but with less emphasis on the thick sauces of traditional French haute-cuisine. The establishment became known as Les Freres Troisgos, earning its first Michelin star in 1955. The hard climb to the prestige of a third star reached its summit in 1968 when French critic Christian Millau gave his view that it was the best restaurant in the world.

It was with some satisfaction that Francois received the news from Zaza that an interview for the apprenticeship had been granted. He was about to meet the Troisgros brothers. It was a moment of excitement, tinged with just a little nervousness. Yet, Francois was a gregarious character and had at least some work-experience from his first job. His training with the local butcher was an indication of his interest and determination. All these experiences, together with the early musical performances as a child in front of crowds were good omens for a confident interview. By bus, the journey to the restaurant would have taken around ninety minutes along a narrow tarmac road. Punctuated with the odd small quaint village, the route held views of beautiful fields and farmhouses. In the event, Zaza drove Francois to the interview. His recommendation was taken seriously by the Troisgros brothers and after a good face to face interview with the candidate, they offered a widely coveted apprenticeship.

"I got the job! The brothers asked a lot of questions and I could tell they were looking to see if I would fit in and whether I had the potential and attitude to work in their establishment. I immediately began to think about how I could get there every day. The journey would take both time and money. I managed to rent the flat above a café - conveniently situated on the opposite side of the street to the restaurant. It felt a little strange at first working away - but at least I got to go home for a day each week. Things were so busy and tiring that there was hardly time to feel homesick."

As a new apprentice, the duties involved working in the kitchen, bar and restaurant. He had to report for work dressed formally in black trousers and a white shirt. The management provided a jacket and black bow tie. It was all part of the plan to display and deliver excellence at every level. Nothing less would be accepted. These standards were embedded in the organisation and all who worked there.

"I had to get up at 5.30 in the morning and serve breakfasts starting at 6am. From 9am, I would clear the dining room in readiness for lunches at mid-day. A 15-minute break was allowed at 10.45

to get changed ready for the lunch service. Before starting work, the waiters would line up for inspection by Marie and Jean Baptiste Troisgros. They carefully checked our appearance – including hair and fingernails. On one occasion, although I'd turned up for the inspection reasonably well-groomed – a single hair was standing up. My colleagues found it quite funny and from that day they nick-named me BuBus – after a wartime cartoon character who was depicted with a single hair standing on his head in the shape of a question-mark."

The staff meant no harm by their nickname. The character they referred to came from a propaganda film "Nimbus Libere" made in wartime Germany for the Vichy French. During the war, French civilians were inadvertently victims of Allied bombing and the Nazis wanted to exploit this tragic fact for propaganda purposes. The war had been long over, but the image of the young cartoon character had remained in memory. In the restaurant, impeccable appearance was at the centre of their desire for excellence. As Francois recalls to his cost, crossing the line of acceptability could have serious consequences:

"On one occasion, my trouser crease wasn't quite up to scratch and I was barred from working at all that day. I was so embarrassed. It felt like a slap in the face. It was a sign that there was no compromise with the supreme standards they had set. "

When she heard about the laundry problem and the importance of proper dress to his job, Francois' landlady offered to do the ironing free of charge. In appreciation, she received regular flowers in return – despite the cost making a significant hole in an already tight budget.

"It was usually a 16-hour day. Although the bosses had a very strong work ethic and demanded full commitment to the job. I found the high standards very satisfying! It spoke about excellence and I wanted to be part of that process."

Francois was initially involved in the thankless but vital basic tasks, essential to any well-run kitchen. Ingredients had to be made ready for the stages that followed, transforming them from raw materials to the dishes that drew clients from all of France and beyond.

"At first, I found myself simply peeling potatoes, preparing vegetables and making ready other ingredients – most of which were sourced locally. They had the be fresh and of the highest quality. Part of my work in the kitchen involved breadmaking. It was all fascinating. The smell of freshly-baked bread was intoxicating. In performing these tasks, I learned the very basics of cooking. The kitchen staff included ten chefs – including the now legendary Guy Savoy who would become one of France's top chefs. Paul Bocuse, who went on to become another cooking legend, was also one of the staff. They would tolerate nothing less than perfection. I felt it an honour to be part of the team."

Bocuse, who died in 2018 in the same room in the restaurant where he was born, had become associated with nouvelle cuisine. He was one of the chefs who would prepare food for the 1969 maiden flight of the Concorde airliner. His career led to the establishment of his own restaurants, including l'Auberge du Pont de Collonges which attained a three-star Michelin rating in 2017. His 3-Star Lyon restaurant facade is a stunning sight with the chef's name displayed in white letters standing tall just above the guttering. High shuttered windows are painted in dark pink with the walls decorated in light green and pink with various culinary graphics set within. At the centre is a stunning sundial in gold, pink and green. Bocuse has demonstrated that making a statement is not always simply confined to the kitchen! Guy Savoy underwent a three-year apprenticeship with the Troisgros brothers and went on to open restaurants in Paris and Las Vegas. The former attained two Michelin stars in 1980. The well-known celebrity chef Gordon Ramsay was trained under Savoy and regarded him as his culinary mentor.

With a small airfield located at Roanne, the Troisgros restaurant was easily accessible for the rich and famous to fly in by light aircraft. Francois recalls serving French-American singer, lyricist and actor Charles Aznavour. Sacha Distel was also a regular visitor and good friend of Jean

Troisgros. The French singing star came to eat around seven times a year. As a waiter, Francois was bound by the strict codes of service, but the visitors were generally friendly towards staff and appreciated their professionalism. During his apprenticeship at the restaurant, the legendary Jean Baptiste Troisgros took Francois under his wing. He confided in the teenager, "You see that prat over there. One day he day, he will be a world-class chef." He was pointing at another apprentice - Bernard Loiseau. Indeed, Loiseau went on to achieve the predicted heights. In 1991, he achieved a coveted three-star Michelin rating. Great attention to detail, frantic work-ethic and discerning palate were his trademarks. He became the only chef to be traded on the Stock Exchange and was awarded numerous national honours by the French government. Tragically, L'oiseau took his own life in 2003. It was rumoured this was due to growing depts and depression. There was a notion that Michelin were about to remove one of the stars in his restaurant's rating. Whilst money was not the prime motivation for working at Troisgros, Francois found the rewards most welcome. After all, there were current travel expenses and he was also at the time still paying instalments on the written-off VeloSoleX!

"The basic salary was proportionate to my age and experience at the time. It was significantly more than I had earned in my first job where I received nothing in tips. From the first day at Troisgros, the staff received a share of the tips from the previous day. This enabled me to have that little extra to pay for the bus trip home for a day each week."

In addition to working in the kitchen, Francois found himself performing duties in the restaurant as a waiter. Guests included the rich and famous, not just from France – but world-wide. The place had become a magnet for tourists, political figures, business travellers and top-of-the-bill entertainment stars. One of the features of dining at the restaurant was the appearance of one of the chefs to sell cigars to the customers at the end of the meal.

"It was interesting to see was the way that the Troisgros family treated the staff. We eat at the restaurant with the bosses. One of the brothers would eat in one sitting with the chefs and the other would eat with the rest of us at another sitting. It was the same menu for all of us. All of the Troisgros family showed every respect for all the team. Having Troisgros on my CV was almost a passport into any kitchen in the world. They had incredibly high-standards in every area of the business – whether it was hygiene, quality of the ingredients, cooking skills, customer service – or value for money. But it also provided me with an opportunity to learn the importance of service in the formula for success. On the one hand, the business of delivering the food in the correct manner was absolutely critical. But that was not all. Each client was an individual personality and came from different backgrounds with differing attitudes and varying temperaments. Judging their mood and how they wanted to engage with their waiter was of great importance and a skill in itself."

The Triosgros brothers recognised that Francois was particularly successful in engaging with the clients. His chatty and friendly manner attracted many complimentary remarks. This was seen as a great asset to the restaurant. As a means of developing this talent to further benefit the restaurant, Marie Troisgros suggested to Francois that he might like to learn a foreign language – with English and German being those most prevalent in terms of foreign visitors. Her plan was to arrange a temporary secondment in one of those countries as a means of attaining competence and developing fluency.

"I was flattered that the restaurant wanted to develop me as an individual. I was attracted to English as I felt that this was an almost universal language. The plan was for me to have a year away learning the language and then to return to Troisgros. The bosses arranged for me to meet Chris Gotelier who was then the manager of the Royal Station Hotel in Hull, East Yorkshire. I had no idea at the time where this was! I met him in Paris. He was looking to recruit staff from France and Italy to work in British Transport Hotels. Although I didn't speak English very well, I had the basics required for taking orders and conducting simple conversations. I recognised that English was an important language and I wanted to become fluent. The intention was to spend one or two years in England and then to return to Troisgros."

The secondment was agreed. Francois began looking forward to the challenge. However, he was a little worried about becoming homesick. Although already spending a lot of time away from home, he was moving to another country. It slowly started to sink in that he would not be able to get back to Bourg Le Thizy every weekend. Yet, he had given the commitment to the restaurant and understood that it was important in terms of career development. He simply had to get on with it. In the period before travelling to Hull, Francois was asked by a friend to help with a few weeks cover at his brasserie in Strasbourg. Although the work was tiring, the long hours were punctuated by celebration evening to mark his friend's birthday. The group travelled by car to a city restaurant. They arrived and parked the vehicle nearby. Inevitably, once inside the establishment, alcohol began to flow. The plan was to leave the car parked-up overnight and collect it later on the next day when the driver was completely sober. Unfortunately the carefully laid plans developed a flaw. Still inside the car, was a surprise present.

The error was discovered only after the meal

was completed. After a short conversation about who should retrieve the gift, Francois found himself nominated to extract it from the vehicle. Although quite intoxicated and hardly able to walk, he grasped the keys and dutifully wobbled-off on his mission. As he lurched along the pavement, swaying precariously, he was unable to fully recall the details of the car. He roughly remembered its colour and make - but had not taken the trouble to note down the registration number. Why would he? In his state of alcohol-induced confusion, they all looked the same. At last, finding a vehicle which roughly resembled the one he thought that he was looking for, Francois attempted to insert the key into the door lock. Unfortunately, there were three reasons this proved a fiddly and unsuccessful mission. In the first place, it was dark. Second, the key wouldn't fit into the lock. Third, although the fact still hadn't dawned, it was the wrong car! At this point, extremely frustrated and eager to return to the festivities, he booted the car door. In a way, it was a cry for help. Help was at hand.

"I felt a tap on my shoulder. When I looked round, a couple of gendarmes were standing there, towering above me. They didn't believe my story. Someone had seen me trying to get into the car– and called the police. A woman was by then hanging out of a nearby window shouting 'It's him.' In reply, I shouted 'silly cow.' Unfortunately, the two gendarmes took a dim view of the situation and put me in a cage in the back of their van and then drove me to the police station. I was put into a cell. They were very unpleasant characters. After that, I was questioned in a room with a light shining in my face. It felt a very aggressive interrogation. I told them the truth about what had happened - but it was no good. It took them until 5pm the next day to sort it all out. It turned out that the woman at the window was the wife of the restauranteur. My boss was at the party and it was he who came to pick me up. There was no damage at all to the car and I was released without any charge or caution."

Whilst in Strasbourg, Francois took a fancy to a Renault 4L car. It was owned by a friend who offered it to him for sale at a very-special price. It was a smallish car of simple design and without frills. Nonetheless, it was an ideal run-around for a man about town. Impressively, French police retained this type of vehicle in their fleet. Some 4Ls were even seen in rallies. Television adverts espoused the vehicle's attributes of comfort, versatility, and luggage capacity. With an impressive fuel consumption, it was filmed effortlessly driving up hills, down kerbs and around mountain tracks. Ideally suited as a family transport, the car was also portrayed in the manufacturer's marketing as being capable of impressing attractive ladies. Francois needed no more persuading. Despite his impending trip, he took the plunge.

"I collected the car from my friend at about 2pm one afternoon and paid him the money. Fifteen minutes later, in a moment of madness, I pulled out in front of another car and it collided with my front passenger door. For a week I drove around with a missing door. It was hopeless as the rain and wind just blew in. I couldn't afford to have it repaired. So, I just drove it to a scrapyard and that was that!"

For all its marketing success and an array of impressive attributes, the Renault 4L had a fundamental unadvertised flaw. Just like the VelosoleX, it was not Francois proof!

TO HULL & NOT BACK

I t was late in 1973 when Francois sailed across the Channel on his journey to Hull and a new job at the city's prestigious Royal Station Hotel. It was his first trip outside France. Travelling north by taxi across the nation's capital, he found himself impressed by what he saw, even though his wonderment was restricted to mere glimpses of the London landmarks he'd seen in picture books and on television. The excitement temporarily masked a growing feeling of homesickness, but he retained a tinge of apprehension for what might lie ahead.

As his connecting train headed North, the wheels clickety-clacked with a rapidly increasing rhythm. The carriage began to rock with the pace of acceleration. At the time, he was travelling into unknown territory. He knew that the Hull was in the north of the country about four hours from London. Beyond that, he had no clue about the city, its people, its rich history or its hinterland. As the verdant countryside drifted past, he continued to ponder about what the future might hold. The immediate aim was to improve his language skills and be able to converse with ease in English. The best way, he'd been advised, was to live and work in the country. So far, without too much trouble, he had successfully bought a coffee and an extremely dubious British Rail sandwich. Eating the curled item was more of a challenge than the act of making the purchase. The taste, he recalled, was disgusting. And it hadn't improved over time despite widespread ridicule on in films, print and on television. Spike Milligan in his comedy show 'Milligna' announced that the long missing Van Gough ear had been found in a British Rail sandwich. Francois was no stranger to such jollity, as in France the SNCF sandwich has a similar reputation. Forewarned was forearmed but in reality it was a case of Hobson's choice - which may account for why, in 1993, during its last year as a public company British Rail sold 8 million of its sandwiches on the railway.

No matter, more palatable culinary delicacies would await the intrepid traveller on arrival in Hull, where he would discover the local favourite chip shop takeaway meal of fish, chips and 'pattie' – which consisted of battered and deep-fried disc-shaped mix of mashed potato and sage seasoning. Chip "butty" sandwiches were also a Hull favourite. Whilst Luftwaffe pilots had the purpose and navigational skills to easily find Hull during World War Two, few people living in the south of England would have had any clue where to precisely locate the city on a map. Its rich fishing heritage and place as a major port were still well-kept secrets. The problem would be only partly addressed in a future Christmas edition of the TV series 'Only Fools & Horses, entitled 'To Hull and Back,' and would be several decades before the city was recognised as the UK City of Culture 2017 - after which it began to appear on TV weather maps. The packed direct train stopped at various stations including the obligatory Doncaster - after which the seating occupancy thinned somewhat. A further hour passed before river views on the outskirts of Hull appeared to the right-hand side of his compartment. He observed that the River Humber was hardly a Mediterranean blue colour. It looked quite brown for some reason.

Although construction of what would temporarily become the world's longest single-span suspension bridge had commenced the previous year, its towers at Hessle on the north bank had not yet risen to become part of the local landscape. As waterfront views gave way to terraced houses alongside the rail-track, the train slowed as it approached its destination. Was this also a destiny for one of the passengers? The squeel of metal wheels on rail track represented but a comma in his wider life story - but a new chapter was about to begin. As the train came to a full stop, Francois gathered his luggage together and alighted on to the platform. The train's motion was replaced by the commotion of passengers heading for the exits and the city air. A little numb in his feelings and with some apprehension, he strode long the platform towards the main concourse. His Station Hotel destination was matter of just a few paces away.

Hull's Paragon station and the adjoining hotel date back to 1848. The architecture represented a superb example of a Victorian railway building. The frontage of the Royal Station Hotel looks on to the busy Ferensway - which was lined with shops, departmental stores and cafes. At the rear, which forms part of the station, guests could step right on to the covered railway concourse . It was in this very location that scenes for Agatha Christie's 'Poirot' film 'The Plymouth Express' were shot in 1991. Five years earlier, John Cleese and Alison Steadman filmed scenes for 'Clockwise' at the Hull Paragon Station. To the sound of echoing arrival announcements on the station tannoy, Francois crossed the concourse and walked straight through a doorway into the hotel building where he would almost immediately commence work. Although, he wasn't aware of it at the time, this was the start of a new life in a friendly city that he would soon call home. The hustle and bustle of the concourse soon faded as he entered the quiet ambiance of the prestigious hotel. He had no immediate opportunity to stroll around and experience the aroma of the city's drains or to converse with a genuine 'cod head' – a title ascribed to the good folk of Hull by the 'yellow bellies' across on the south bank of the river. Rather, it was the familiar accent of a compatriot in the hushed hotel lobby that extended the first hand of friendship.

"Mr Gotelier welcomed me and showed me to my temporary room in the hotel. I was given a month to find accommodation. Luckily, I quickly managed to rent a flat in Park Street which was just a few minutes away on foot. My initial job was to work as a waiter serving food in the main restaurant upstairs. I began doing breakfast, lunch and evening meals with banqueting. The restaurant was closed at weekends."

Soon afterwards, Francois found himself working in the 'Brigantine' restaurant which was located on the hotel's ground floor and serving both French and English food. His job as barman was dispensing cocktails and drinks. The other staff were all girls. And whilst this may have been the equivilant of giving a child the keys to a candy store, there was barely enough time to view the treasures on display - let alone dabble in their delights. The naming of the restaurant may have been a nod to the Hull's long nautical history– the word 'brigantine' referring to a sailing vessel. After a couple of months, the restaurant was renamed 'La Caravelle' to emphasise the French aspect of its cuisine. The French word 'caravelle' translates as being a light sailing ship – so the nautical connection with the city was maintained. At the helm was a French chef assisted by an Italian head waiter. There was a mixed staff of Italian,

Greek, German and English waiters. It was a very high-class operation serving hotel guests and local business customers. Pay days were always welcome - but rarely greeted with excessive joy. The role was not highly remunerated. As the days and weeks drifted-by, Francois began to settle into the work routine. His thoughts began to turn more seriously towards financial considerations and his desire to return home to France whenever possible.

"There were times when other hotels in the group offered extra hours - so I decided to take up these opportunities. The railway fare was always free. If I took leave to return home to France, my tickets were provided free on British Railways – and also on the French railways. On the downside, my salary was just eighteen pounds per month. Due to the 6am start, staff were allowed free breakfast when working - but not lunch or evening meals. At least the hotel provided me with a jacket to wear. On my evenings off, I would go to Tony's, a nearby pub in Albermarle Street where I played as a resident drummer. Other artists would come in and play and I would provide the backing. Since I worked mainly breakfast and lunch, I had quite a lot of evenings off. Johnny Pat (Patterson), a well-known music legend in Hull would often come in with his guitar and sing. Whilst working at the hotel, I met several stars who had been performing at the Hull New Theatre and City Hall. Stephane

Grapelli was one who was a guest at the hotel and would sit on the stool and chat for hours. I got on well with him because we were fellow countrymen and shared an interest in music. Hank Marvin, Cliff Richard and the Shadows also frequented the bar and I found them very friendly and chatty. Although they would be mixing with our ordinary customers, aside from general pleasantries, the stars were allowed their own space and privacy. They were ordinary, but talented people, who were very well known. Obviously, they had a passionate fan base who might have caused some disruption had they know that they were guests at the hotel. Before my year's contract at the Royal Station Hotel was finished, I was approached by David Allison who had The Bake House in Car Lane. It was a bakery. I agreed to open a restaurant in the basement as his employee. We called it Chez Francois. There had been a similar operation involving somebody else - but they had gone off to establish their own business. The arrangement suited both of us perfectly."

At that stage in his career, Francois was not an experienced chef. He'd picked up the basics of food preparation at Les Freres Troisgros and had been involved a little in cooking – but this opportunity was really a matter of being thrown in at the deep end. The job involved full-time responsibility for cooking in the kitchen and the supervision of a team of waiters and a commis chef to do food preparation, starters, desserts – and washing up. He did have the opportunity to develop the menu and found it very interesting - but challenging.

"I decided to base the food on dishes that had been offered by my grandma in her establishment and on some of the dishes from Les Freres Troisgros. Notably, I think I think was the first one in the region, or certainly in Hull, to offer frogs legs and snails as they should be done! The restaurant was always busy and I met some really nice people. Hull is a very friendly city."

Jacques Meilhan, a native of Brittany came to Hull in 1969 aged 19 years. He'd met Lynne, a Hull girl, whilst on holiday in Jersey. Their friendship blossomed and they were married shortly afterwards, making their home in East Yorkshire. For Jacques, the appearance of a French restaurant in the centre of Hull was an opportunity too good to miss. He simply had to go along. At Chez Francois, Jacques discovered a fellow countryman. The visit was not simply the first step in what would become a lifelong friendship, but it immediately brought a touch of France back into his life. Memories of home flooded back. Thanks to three years training as a butcher when he'd been in his teens, Jacques could cast a professional eye on the quality of the meat on offer.

"It was clear from those early days that Francois wanted everything to be right. He strived for perfection. He was desperate for success, but he had every patience towards his customers. That's what made him tick. He wanted to please people and loved it when they were happy with the food and service."

After completing a year of national service in the French military, Jacques had returned to the Hull area. He then began working for a flooring company, then owned by his father in -law. Ultimately, he would lead the organisation into a period of unprecedented growth and recognition on an international scale. With other business interests, at the peak of success, Jacques had a large number of employees on his payroll. A quietly spoken yet dynamic character, Jacques would later play an important role in Francois' career. After a year, David Allison offered to sell Francois the Carr Lane business. It had been successful, but probably not enough to justify his investment. Francois went to see his bank manager who offered to lend him the money. However, he decided to take advice from his family.

"I discussed the proposition with my mother who reminded me of the pitfalls of borrowing. As a family, we had avoided going in to dept because of the cost of credit. On that advice, I decided not to take up the offer."

Declining the opportunity to buy the business at a time when the owner wanted to move-on had its own dynamic. There was an urgent need to consider pastures new. By this time, Francois had met

Sue, the woman who would later become his wife. Thoughts of permanently returning to France had all but evaporated and his future seemed to be in East Yorkshire. This led inevitably to questions on how he would continue to earn a living in the hospitality industry. As regularly happens in life, Francois discovered that, as one door closes, another can soon open. Sue's mum worked in the canteen at the University of Hull. She knew of a vacancy that had arisen at the Grange Park Hotel in the nearby village of Willerby - a quiet and pleasant suburb just to the west of the city. The owner Ted Avery also had the Newland Park Hotel in Cottingham Road, Hull. After applying for the post, Francois was offered and accepted the job of head waiter. Surrounded by 12 acres of landscaped gardens, in the mid-seventies, The Grange Park, as it was then known, was a prestigious hotel and restaurant situated on the north west outskirts of Willerby.

Franco Ciuffatelli, an Italian, had originally worked at the hotel as head waiter. Firmly of the 'old school' he was now the highly respected restaurant manager. In him, Francois found a fellow spirit when it came to ensuring that supreme standards of service and the highest levels of customer satisfaction were maintained. The two shared a mutual respect and a joint approach to maintaining the high reputation already earned by the restaurant. After a few months, Franco moved on to take up a post at the Westfield Country

Club and Francois found himself immediately pro-moted to the role of restaurant manager. It was a magnificent opportunity to develop his already blossoming career. He took the chance with both hands and especially relished working with the universally popular hotel owner Ted Avery.

"In those days, the manager was in charge. I dic-tated what happened throughout the restaurant. In that field of operations, I had total control. My relationship with the hotel owner was fantastic. He was popular with everyone because he knew how to treat people and they responded in turn. I was happy at the Grange Park Hotel."

The restaurant opened at lunchtime and then again for a period from 6pm. Serving both hotel guests and the discerning public, it was open seven days a week. The kitchen employed up to a dozen staff under the head chef. Customers were served by around three waiters under a new head waiter. Given the restaurant's standing, the employment of a specialist wine waiter was essential. At the centre of the operation, Francois was in his elem-ent. In the space of just a few short years, he had risen into a senior management position in a high-quality restaurant.

"It was my job to hire and fire restaurant staff – although dismissal was absolutely the last resort. It was rarely necessary and always regrettable. I had under me a team of professionals. They were of an excellent standard, thanks to careful recruitment. One of the team was Shane Whitfield – son of the star Hull singer David Whitfield. He was an excellent chef, always in a good mood and blessed with a great sense of humour."

Francois' working day was influenced to a large extent by his enthusiasm and workaholic tendencies. Arriving at 9am, meetings with staff were an essential part of ensuring continuing motivation and the maintenance of standards in the restaurant. Whilst the head chef and wine waiter did the buying for their respective departments, purchases had to be signed-off by one of the hotel's managers as a part of overall financial control. It was Francois' job to ensure that the waiting staff operated up to the required standard both individually and as a team. His approach to the team was reminiscent of that he had experienced as a teenager at the Roanne restaurant - Les Freres Troisgros. Staff under Francois were expected to be at the level required of a top restaurant. Nothing less would do. This meant immaculate appearance, impeccable manners and a totally professional standards of service. He was always seen as a perfectionist by clients of the restaurant. In addition to having an attractive menu, beautifully cooked food, good value and exceptional customer service it was necessary to ensure total quality in every level. Glasses had to be perfectly clean and shining. All the silver cutlery had to be sparkling at every serving. Each day, the silver would be cleaned in a special machine. Salt and pepper pots would be emptied and refilled.

"Things didn't always go to plan. We hosted a lot of Jewish events at the hotel. I remember on one occasion that the rabbi asked for a sandwich. There was a mix-up with the order and it wasn't immediately realised they had used a ham filling instead of the requested turkey. We were horrified, but the mistake wasn't detected by the customer who later remarked to the waiter that it was the tastiest sandwich he had ever eaten!"

In addition to being a large and well-appointed hotel, the Grange Park boasted substantial grounds. When visiting the area, the hotel was a natural stopover for celebrities coming to perform at shows in the area. Amongst the stars were the Bay City Rollers. The pop idols flew in by helicopter prior to their show at the ABC theatre in Hull City Centre. Francois recalls that they were a pleasant group of young lads who were incessantly cracking jokes. Customers in the restaurant included many prominent people in business and commerce either as visiting guests at the hotel or as residents in the Hull and East Riding area.

❋ ❋ ❋

One regular local businessman who had long-admired Francois' abilities was Mr Charles Townend – owner of the House of Townend retail and wholesale wine business. His son John

Townend was an MP at the time. Already successful in the wine trade, the family operated thirty-
five wine shops as part of their business portfolio.
The House of Townend retail wine brand was
iconic in the Hull and East Yorkshire area and beyond. Unbeknown to Francois, the Townend em-
pire was eyeing up the potential purchase of the
rival Willerby business - Hotel Eden.

The takeover was the brainchild of Derek Baugh
– a chef of some considerable repute, having
worked at London's Dorchester Hotel. On the
promise of an ambitious future restaurant project,
Baugh had been persuaded to leave his role leading
a catering course at Hull College. In an inspired
move, John Townend had swooped to recruit the
chef, initially to run a restaurant at The Nag's Head
pub at Routh. In a relatively short space of time, it
became one of the few genuine quality restaurants
in the East Riding of Yorkshire and quickly established a reputation for fine food. From a teach-
ing role, amounting to ten hours a week, Baugh
had been projected into a position that consumed
many times the hours of the earlier academic commitment! Yet, it was a labour of love in a can-
do, dynamic organisation, where the grass did not
grow around the feet of directors.

After three years at the Nag's Head, Derek Baugh
pressed the owner to be as good as his word and
to deliver him a more challenging project. He recommended that the company contact the owner

of the Hotel Eden in Willerby. Built in 1890 and later extended, what was originally known as the Manor House was rumoured not to be doing too well and was to be put up for sale. It offered a superlative platform to build upon the sucesses at The Nag's Head. The initial approach from the Townend Group, which came in the mid-1970's was firmly rebuffed. However, despite that flat refusal, a deal was successfully completed within just a few weeks. A curious part of the sale was that the principal vendor could remain as a resident in one of the hotel rooms and be fed free of charge! Appointed to head up the new venture as Managing Director, Derek set about recruiting a team that could deliver success across the entire Hotel.

The transfer of operations did not go as smoothly as had been hoped. Baugh had some challenges in resetting the hotel culture and attitudes to his liking. This was only achieved by adjusting the personnel profile such that after three months, only one of the original team was left. As part of the rebranding, the hotel was renamed The Willerby Manor. It was, in part, a way of advertising the fact that the hotel had changed hands. A new broom was in the process of sweeping the place clean. Francois had contacts that alerted him to the possibility of a more interesting and better paid role. It was perfect timing. After an interview, he was offered the job of restaurant manager working with the skilful kitchen team that was already in post.

In this new position, Francois was his own boss with increased salary, flexible hours and a high level of autonomy within his department. Answering directly to Baugh, he assumed control of the restaurant operations. This involved hiring staff, ensuring high standards of service, greeting clients, taking food orders in the restaurant, training, discipline - and a raft of associated tasks. For Francois, that was as good as things could ever get. He had a very well-paid employment with total job satisfaction, working in an organisation where there was complete harmony with colleagues - and excellent relations with customers. It was, at once - Utopia, Heaven and Nirvana all in one.

"In the period of over 16 years that I spent at Willerby Manor, I was given the space and respect to operate within my remit. Mr Baugh was the best boss I ever experienced in my entire employed career. Having worked at a top Hotel in London, he was a chef in his own right and knew everything there was to know about cooking and hotel management. He was a master."

Although the front of house operation under Francois always operated brilliantly, at one point during his tenure, the restaurant's financial performance dipped as a result of menu changes instigated by Derek Baugh who recalls the period clearly:

"Francois was absolutely brilliant running the front of house department. The customers loved him. He was a real draw and he established fantastic relationships with the clients. Business was turned round within a month of his arrival and clients quadrupled in number. I decided to become involved as the lead chef developing some new menus. With Francois in the restaurant and a new French Restaurant branding, things went from strength to strength - and into profitability. I wanted to keep abreast of the times and eventually spent a week or so in London working in a friend's top restaurant serving Nouvelle Cuisine. Francois was a bit sceptical about this from the off. When I came back and tried the new recipes in an East Yorkshire setting it was a disaster! In the end, I decided to revert to more authentic French dishes after a regular client bluntly told me he'd been all over the world in restaurants and never eaten peas in a pod before. He said we were serving trash and stopped coming!"

Nouvelle Cusine had been developed and championed by the Troigross family back in Roanne and whilst Francois held that fresh ingredients locally sourced were at the heart of great cooking in any menu or style, he'd realised that in its purest form there might be problems with some local clients who were less open to the sudden changes in style and in some cases – any changes at all! For Baugh, it was all part of trying to offer choice, quality and style to clients. Yet, he was wise enough to realise that the client has the ultimate say on whether the menu choices are acceptable

"We were all a great team at the Willerby Manor. We'd have been dead in the water without Francois running front of house in the restaurant. His French accent gave a great gravitas to running a French style kitchen. He is ebullient, friendly and has a great sense of humour."

The mutual respect between Francois and Derek shines through in what Francois recalls of those times:

"I was completely happy because I had no burning desire to work in the kitchen. Although I had skills as a chef, I relished the management side and having contact with the public. Our restaurant team included around 5 full-time staff and several part-timers. Many of them were French. I had advertised in local media in the Roanne region of France where I had originated. They had good English language skills and came with top class training at a French catering school. We had exceptional banqueting chefs able to handle the pressure and demands of large-scale catering. Teamwork was exceptional and people with the highest standards were being brought to the restaurant to work. Supreme quality was the aim, expectation and outcome. The restaurant had high scores in the Egon Ronay Guide."

Francois remains extremely complimentary about the team at Willerby Manor. Many were drafted in from France to provide authenticity - and for their work ethic and culinary skills.

“They were the best team I have ever worked alongside. Ariel went on to be a wine-maker in France, Mirielle and Eric Fremiot later went to Raymond Blank OBE at Le Manoir Aux Quat’Seasons. Later he came back to Willerby as restaurant manager. The last time I heard, he was in Japan as the General Manager of two restaurants."

In March 2011, Eric had found himself featured in the French media 'Le Journal' after Japan experienced the strongest earthquake in its history. The magnitude 9 earthquake was a natural disaster which instigated a tsunami and major nuclear accident at a power station on the coast. Two hundred square miles of coastal land were flooded. Eric who was in Tokushima, 400km south of Tokyo, reported to his anxious family that he had barely felt the tremors. Back in France, his mother was inundated with enquiries from friends and neighbours who were concerned about his safety.

* * *

Friday 3 February 1978 was the day that Jimmy Carter met Anwar Sadat in Washington DC to discuss the Middle east peace process. Australia beat India on the 6th day of the final test - with India being dismissed for 445 runs after chasing 493 to win. Closer to home it was wedding day for Francois and Sue. Never one to skimp, the dashing groom had arranged the reception for 100 guests at the famous Gainsboro Fish and Chip restaurant in Hull city centre. The ceremony was held at Beverley Registry Office. On the way to the ceremony, the car overheated and boiled over, causing a frantic race to get there on time.

"We were short of cash and didn't want to bust the bank. I couldn't afford to bring my family over for the wedding - so it was really all Sue's side that attended. It was impossible for me to take any time off from the restaurant for honeymoon and in truth, I could hardly afford to be off at all in those days!"

In the early years of marriage, the couple's financial situation gradually improved to the extent that they were able to take holidays abroad twice a year – often in the South of France with Jaques Mielhan. Usually Francois and Sue would go their own way during the day and meet up with the other couple in the evenings. Whilst staying at the Hotel Roi Soleil en-route to Provence, the group met for dinner. Francois and Sue were always first to the bar.

"We had dressed casually for dinner at the hotel. Sue and I were having a drink at the bar. I was in casual trousers and a quite distinctive patterned holiday shirt I had bought from an outfitter in Willerby. As Jaques and his wife appeared, I noticed straight away that we were wearing exactly the same shirts! Due to the outlandish design, it was obvious that it was a lash-up. We laughed about it and I quickly went and got changed!"

On the last day of their stay at the hotel, Francois had £700 stolen from the safe in the room. They had stayed there regularly over many years and knew the owners very well. They did not want to involve the police as any adverse publicity would damage the hotel's reputation. It was agreed that, as compensation, it would not be necessary to pay the hotel bill. It was agreed that the parties would keep in touch and it was later revealed that thefts were discovered being carried out by a boy who was going out with a chambermaid. The experience did not cause lasting damage and the hotel remained a destination in future visits to the area. On such a return visit, Francois decided to drive to a local bar for a drink. On the excursion, he had a long conversation with some friendly police officers. On his return to the hotel, the electric gates malfunctioned and caused damage to the front of the hire car. The following morning, he bumped into the same officers.

"The cops were great and sympathised with my predicament. They knew that the car hire firm would make a hugely disproportionate charge for repairs. I was surprised when they told me to follow them. We drove for twenty miles to a garage and they had a chat with the owner who repaired the car totally free of charge! When I returned it to the hire company, they walked round it and signed off the bond refund with no problem!"

Unfortunately, The French connection did not always work so well. In 1493, navigator Christopher Columbus had been the first European to venture upon Guadaloupe. Centuries later, Francois and Sue holidayed upon its shores and were almost immediately confronted by a bandit demanding money as they left the hotel. Luckily, an armed hotel guard intervened and scared off the would-be attacker. Ride-by thefts were commonplace as youngsters on bikes grabbed handbags from pedestrians and threw them to accomplices in vehicles. Guards were unable to act until the thefts had occurred and so prevention was difficult. Other dangers and annoyances in the area included occasional island-wide strikes and mosquitoes carrying the Zika virus and dengue fever.

After hiring a car on the island, Francois & Sue decided to visit a teacher friend who lived in a nearby village. As he entered a filling station to top up on fuel, they saw a group of men speaking to a woman driver who was at a petrol pump. They appeared to be causing her some distress. A passenger in her car got out to confront the men and as he did so one of the group aimed a pistol at him. A shot rang out and the man fell to the ground fatally wounded. The men then drove off at speed.

"We were in shock. The police soon arrived. We left our details and went straight back to the hotel. Unfortunately, there was not all that much comfort there. Later in the day we found lizards all over the inside walls. A friend assured us that they would be gone in the morning. Later we were spending time with the next-door guests at the hotel when we heard a noise from our room. We thought at first it was the wind. We went to investigate and disturbed burglars who ran off. The hotel was on top of rocks next to the sea with a sheer drop below. The window was wide open. They had climbed the rocks to get inside our room and had made off with money and some belongings. The next day, the hotel owner came to see us. The police had been involved and it was discovered that the hotel guards had been part of the plot to rob guests. The criminal gang was also being supported by a receptionist who was passing information about the guests and their movements. We kept in touch with the French owner and translated some of his menus into English, but there is no way we would go back. Tourists from cruise ships were being followed by bandits and this actually happened to us. We told a police officer and pointed out the men. They were known to the officer and as he approached, they ran off."

Holidays in the South of France were always a treat – with Provence being a popular destination. The location was also popular with many rich and famous personalities, some of whom had properties in the area – including actor Joan Thaw (The Sweeney & Inspector Morse). Thaw was the star of the TV series 'A Year in Provence' based on the 1989 book by best-selling author Peter Mayle. One day whilst shopping in a local market, Francois heard a familiar English voice. It was that of Inspector Jack Regan – posing as actor John Thaw!

"We were amongst the stalls in the town's market when I heard a voice I recognised. As I turned to look, I saw that it was John Thaw dressed in casual gear. As I stared at him in partial disbelief, he simply smiled and judging that I was French said "Bonjour!" His wife Sheila Hancock was browsing through the stalls and shopping. We shook hands and had a conversation in English for over half an hour. He was interested to learn that I worked in East Yorkshire! A week later, we were back in the market again having a look around. Suddenly, I heard someone say, 'Bonjour Francois! It was John Thaw again. He was a lovely person. A star - but totally grounded."

Francois and Sue pictured on holiday in Bourg-le-Thizy

Francois was never far away from bumping into

someone famous. During one holiday in France, he stayed at Hotel La Columb D'Or (The Golden Dove) in Saint-Paul de Venice. He began chatting with a distinguished gentleman and his lady during a game of boules. Suddenly realising who the pair were, Francois was not in the least bit phased by the couple's global fame. However, his mother Juliette - who was also in the holiday party - was speechless, tembling and awe-struck! Actor Yves Montand, who owned a property in the village, was her film favourite! Simone Signoret, Montand's film-star wife was also present - and the group chatted freely on a day that Juliette would never forget. In 1991, Montand died of a heart attack on the set of a film in which he played a character who died of a heart attack. He'd earlier appeared in the film 'Let's Make Love,' with Marilyn Monroe. The press alleged that he and his co-star had conducted an affair off-set. On another occasion, whilst holidaying in the small village of Le Castellet in Avignon, Provence, Francois was in the local photo shop talking casually to the owner.

"He suddenly said, 'Oh look who is here. My friend!' I turned round and saw a flash car that had drawn up outside. Out jumped someone who looked very much like Mick Jagger. I saw that inside the car was Ronny Wood and Jerry Hall. It was indeed Mick Jagger walking into the store! He collected his photos and we all had a chat for a few minutes. He had the impression that Hull was a bit of a dump - but I put him right on that one!

UP & DOWN UNDER

Working as restaurant manager, Francois had direct contact with most of the diners. To them, he represented the restaurant. That face to face interaction could make the difference between success and failure. A friendly relationship with very satisfied clients led to some diners showing their appreciation in a variety of ways. On one occasion, the directors and players of both Hull's professional rugby clubs had attended for a joint dinner. When they discovered he was from rugby hot-bed Roanne, it was if a lightbulb had been switched on. Although he was not a big rugby league fan at that time, Francois accepted sudden invitations from both clubs to attend a game. He was flattered and open to sample the match day atmosphere to see if it would be something that interested him. It did.

"At the dinner at Willerby Manor, both club chairmen asked me about where I was from. When I replied 'Roanne,' they knew that it was a region in France where rugby was popular. Hull KR Chairman Bill Land and Hull FC chairman Charlie Watson both asked me to go to a match and provided me with complimentary hospitality tickets. I went to see both teams and really enjoyed the experience. The first game I went to see was at Craven Park when Hull *KR* played at the Holderness Road ground. It was hard to get parked and I had to walk a long way from where I had left my car. When I arrived, I was treated like a king. The match was great to watch. The players were from working backgrounds and really got stuck in. It mattered to them. After the game I was introduced to the players and staff – including Phil Lowe, Roger Millward, Clive Sullivan, Steve Hartley, David Watkinson and others. I'd already seen Clive Sullivan on TV play in an International game in France. He scored a magnificent try that was probably the best in the tournament. He was well known in France."

The following week, Francois attended a game at rival club Hull FC. Remarkably, the rivalry between the clubs seemed to transcend that which they shared on the field. Not to be outdone by KR, Hull FC set their stall out in fine style to impress. Francois was most impressed.

"Roy Waudby was the Vice Chairman of Hull FC in those days. He knew Sue's family and knew a friend of mine as well. He gave me an envelope. Inside I found three tickets for me, Sue and son. Also, inside was a car park pass - so that I didn't have to walk far to get to the game. Roy winked and told me that Hull FC knew how to look after its customers. I watched the game from great seats, was treated to a half-time drink and experienced amazing hospitality after the game – including meeting all the players. I loved the match and really liked Hull's style of play. I became a fan. Sue's family were FC fans – so it was probably a wise decision on my part anyway!"

Later, Francois was presented with a complimentary season pass by Roy. Now a friend of the club, Francois was only too delighted to assist when it came to attracting players from France. There was a beautiful symmetry to the arrangement as Francois recalls:

"The club asked me to speak to some of the French players they wanted to sign. I would ring them and do my best to sell the club and the area - so that they would want to come to the city. I was involved in the process of signing Patrick Solal who was a French winger. Patrick Entat was another successful transfer. In his case, I went over to Nice airport to get his signature. I promised that I would help him when he came over. We are still friends to this day."

Patrick Entat played in the France rugby league team. Francois was torn in his allegiance when it came to international matches against England. He tried to sit on the fence - but may have inadvertently affected the result of an international, thanks to a mischievous sense of humour.

"Patrick was as tough as they come but decided he wanted a dog. You might have thought he'd choose something very macho, but instead he paid a great deal of money for a fluffy white Bichon Frise dog. They are very cute and almost like cuddly toys. One day he took the dog for a walk and let it off the lead. Unfortunately, it was immediately run over by a car. Shortly afterwards, France were due to play Great Britain. Roy Waudby was in the official party for the game. I gave him a sealed envelope to pass on to Patrick when he shook hands with all the players at the start of the game before the national anthems. When it came to it, Roy shook hands with Patrick and told him he had an envelope on him from me and that he'd pass it on after the game. Patrick insisted on reading it there and then on the pitch. As he read the note he laughed and uttered some unprintable expletives."

The note written by Francois said: 'You dog killer. You should be locked up. That poor dog. Still don't worry Patrick, have a good match.' The note was intended as a friendly wind-up - and it was taken in the right way.

"When Patrick next met up with me later, we had a laugh about the note. He was a key player and he told me that he'd been thinking about the poor dog all the match. France lost by 40 or 50 points! Roy was the driving force in trying to get players into the club. We weren't always successful. Jean Piere Rives was a scrum half and Serge Blanco a France full-back. Neither player wanted to come because of the bad weather over in England. Maybe I should have tried harder and explained about the great French food at Willerby Manor Restaurant!"

✽ ✽ ✽

On an evening off from duties at the hotel, Francois and Sue attended a concert at the Bridlington Spa starring French heart-throb Sacha Distel. The singer epitomised French charm. Good-looking and sophisticated, he famously declined a marriage proposal from French actress Bridget Bardot with whom he'd had a short relationship. He later married Olympic skier Francine Breaud. The audience was enthralled by the singer's polished performance. From his catalogue of songs, 'Raindrops Keep Falling on My Head,' reached number ten in the UK Hit Parade. In the interval at the concert, Francois spoke with an American who was part of the star's entourage. Sacha had been a friend of Francois' former boss Jean Troisgros and a regular visitor at the restaurant at Roanne. Sacha was a huge show business personality in France. He was one of many 'A List' stars to come to the restaurant which was one of the first to attain 3 Michelin stars. That reputation drew people not just from France - but from around the world. As a friendly waiter, Francois soon became popular with the clientele.

"I spoke with the American at the bar. He seemed to be a road manager. I suggested to him that Sacha might remember me from my time at the restaurant in France. I asked if it might be possible to have a chat with him. The man went off and came back to the bar. He reported that Sacha would be delighted to meet me in his dressing room at the end of the show. Sue and I met up with the gentleman at a prearranged spot in the theatre and he escorted us to meet Sacha. Sue was in a bit of a daze, not really believing it was happening! As soon as I walked in the room, he leapt up and greeted me with a handshake, smile and the trademark sparkling eyes. He greeted me with the words, 'Hey Bubus.' This was the nickname that I'd acquired at Les Freres Troigros. He'd remembered. The reunion was a great success and the conversation turned to my current role as restaurant manager at the Willerby Manor Hotel. Sacha told me that he and his entourage had largely been eating cold food on the tour so far. The show finished late and hotel kitchens were invariably closed by the time the final curtain came. He never ate a big meal before the show. At that time, their hotel was in York – so there was no chance they would provide hot food at such a late hour. I rang Derek Baugh at the Willerby Manor. I told him that I was with Sacha Distel and his entourage of about 30 people and asked if we could lay on steak, chips and salad done the French way. At first, he thought it was a wind-up. Sacha came with me and Sue in my car and the musicians and roadies followed in the tour bus. My own car was actually in for some repairs and the courtesy car they gave me was a Skoda.

In those days, it was frowned on as a bit of a joke car. Imagine, international superstar Sacha Distel being driven away from the venue in a Skoda!"

On arrival at Willerby Manor at around midnight, the surprise guests were pleased to find the hot food all ready. Francois rolled up his sleeves to provide the service and it was like being back in Roanne all over again. To add to the magic of the occasion, the hotel's night porter saw his opportunity to be discovered and gave the audience a song on his acoustic guitar. Royally fed, watered and entertained, Sacha and his crew paid the bill and headed off for York at about 4 am. After a long illness, Sacha Distel sadly died, aged 71, on 22 July 2004. Extolled in the French press as a family man, he was still fond of being in the company of girls. He once said, 'Just because you are on a diet, it doesn't mean you can't look at the menu.' Looking back, Francois was full of praise for the star:

"He didn't need to meet me at the Spa. It was late in the evening and he was tired. I had only been a waiter at Les Freres Troisgros. Yet, he made the time. He and my former boss Jean Troisgros were very good friends, so I guess that was one reason he made the effort. Having said that, he was well-mannered, approachable and willing to do something out of the ordinary. It is a great memory."

Francois recalls meeting football star Billy Bremner at the hotel. The Scot was a Leeds United legend and Scotland international. Known for his biting tackles, battling character and no-nonsense approach, Bremner joined Hull City towards the end of his football career. Signed by Hull manager, John Kaye, Bremner had met club representatives at the hotel to discuss a possible deal. In attracting players to the club, the directors realised that impression management was important. Creating an impression was not always an acceptable act - especially in front of guests in the breakfast dining area. So when a member of the Showaddywaddy band attempted to enter wearing only a towel, Francois had to step in and politely advise rearding a suitable dress code.   Whilst a little bit of soap might not have washed away his tears, luckily the pop star was not too offended!

Given that the hotel had changed its name from Hotel Eden to Willerby Manor, the arrival of famous singer Frankie Vaughan was testimony to a missed marketing opportunity. Of his 80 easy listening and traditional singles, 'Garden of Eden' was one of his more notable hits. Readers of a certain age, will not fail to remember 'Give me the Moonlight, Give me the Girl,' as his party piece. Conducting business in beautiful surroundings and with good service and excellent food was always a good way to proceed. The hotel's charms were not lost on other visitors to the area, some of whom arrived by unconventional means. Noel Edmonds is a well-known writer, producer and TV presenter who first became known as a disk jockey on Radio Luxembourg. Amongst his many talents,

Edmonds is a licenced helicopter pilot. One of his aircraft had a personalised registration G-NOEL.

"Noel wanted to fly in by helicopter, but we did not have a landing pad – so we improvised by laying out a bed sheet held down by rocks. I had the opportunity to have a long one to one chat with him. He was very friendly and down to earth. At his next gig, he mentioned to the audience that he had stayed with Francois at the Willerby Manor Hotel. Not all publicity costs a fortune!"

Derek Baugh recalls singer Cliff Richard as a guest at the hotel. The star was performing in Hull and arrived late in the evening. This made it easier to shield him from the public who had either left or were in their rooms at that time. Derek recalls an ad-hoc photo session arranged with the special guest.

"Cliff readily agreed to have his photo taken with me. As we posed, I asked if he felt embarrassed having to stand with an old chap like me. Cliff smiled and said not to worry, he wasn't that far behind me. Our ages weren't that different - but he looked so young."

Although the hotel hosted many famous guests, aside from any security requirements or special circumstances, all guests were treated in the same way – a point Derek makes seriously:

"We treated everybody the same. They are all paying customers and as such are entitled to the same treatment. Sometimes you see restauranteurs spending most of their time with diners they know. That isn't fair. It is important to give everyone the same respect and time."

* * *

Francois and Sue decided to take a holiday in Australia. His relationship with Hull FC had meant that he'd made many friends on the playing staff and the management team and was hoping to renew some of these relationships on the visit. In normal circumstances, the trip would have stretched the purse strings somewhat, but a piece of good fortune had come their way. Some-time earlier, at a club function at the Willerby Manor, a club representative had sold Francois tickets for a lottery - with the draw to be made at half-time at the next home game. His connection with the club was well-known to many fans. When the draw was made, it became clear that the owner of ticket 801 was Francois Primpied. In good humour, a section of the fans chanted "Fix, fix, fix." In fact, the windfall of £1000 had got him out of a fix!

On the stop-off in Singapore, Sue and Francois stayed in the President Merlin Hotel and set off to experience some of the sights in the city. When returning to the hotel, there was no sign of a taxi, so they decided to take a rickshaw as several riders were offering their services.

For comfort reasons, it was decided that Francois and Sue would ride separately as the carriages were not so generous in width. One of the rider's was fat and the other quite thin. Francois had the dubious honour of being pedalled by the heavier of the two. When it came to a steep hill, Sue's rickshaw effortlessly raced on ahead. Frustrated, Francois called for more effort so that they could keep up. Faced with a sweating, panting and slowly expiring rider, he suggested that they swap places:

"He had the cheek to tell me that I was too fat to pull up the hill. I told him the problem was that it was he who was too fat to cycle up the hill. In the end, I ended up pedalling him, at one point going through a red light! He just sat in the back giving me directions. When we arrived, they tried to overcharge us by a ridiculous amount. I offered a quarter of what they were asking as it had been me who had done most of the work anyway. They were not happy, so I told them that I would call the police. At that, they both sped off without taking any money at all!"

On arrival in Australia, Francois and Sue were met at the airport by a squad of rugby players and some of their wives. It was great to renew past friendships. The players had received the benefit of help in Hull during their playing days in the area and were now keen to reciprocate the favours. The reception party included Peter Sterling and Geoff Gerard. During the stay down-under the pair went to see several rugby games. At one of the matches, purely by chance, they bumped into John White who was the Honorary President of Hull FC. He had been Peter Sterling's agent- a player thought by many to be the best number 7 ever signed by the club. Sterling had been instrumental in arranging a large part of the hospitality afforded to Francois and Sue.

"John White explained that he had business ties in Australia. It was a chance meeting. Back in Hull, I'd had made friends with Dick Gemmel – another of the Hull FC legends. After a few minutes, who should roll up but Dick Gemmel! It was just a great day out."

The players decided to treat Sue and Francois to a meal at The Bush Restaurant. Australia-style, the food was mixed grills with meat heavily repre-sented on the menu. The place had a large function room and after the meal, the players decided to put Francois on the spot. In fact, in front of an audi-ence of 150 people, he found himself thrust into the spotlight. Called on to the stage as a 'Welcome to Australia' moment, he was jokingly asked by the band whether he would like to join them. It was an offer that they did not expect to be taken-up! Yet to the surprise of the performers and the audience, Francois accepted the invitation. He got to his feet, confidently climbed on the stage and took over a lagerphone that was being used by a bandsman. A makeshift instrument, it is made typically with a broom handle with beer bottle tops loosely nailed along its length. Another shorter length of broom handle has furniture tacks nailed on. Sounds are made by shaking and stamping the long piece on the floor and by striking or stroking with the short length (bow). As the band began to play, Francois gave a credible accompaniment on the unfamiliar bush instrument. The audience loved it. But more shocks were to follow. As the applause subsided, he asked if he could have a go on the drums. This was the showman in his element. With everyone apart from Sue expecting an amateur crash, bang wallop performance, the professional standard drumbeats took everyone by surprise. The players who had set him up in good spirit were left sitting agog – but delighted that the tables had been turned in such an entertaining way.

Whilst down-under, the plan had been to hire a car. However, there was a shortage of petrol at the time and the vehicle was hardly used. Due to the low mileage, they received some refund on the deal. In any case, they were shown great hospitality by the professional rugby family and were taken everywhere by various players and their wives. As part of the kindnesses shown, they met the owner and were shown round the premises of top rugby league publication in Sydney. Thereafter, copies of the magazine were sent by post to Francois in the UK.

"It was a wonderful visit and the players did us

proud. We visited many restaurants. At the time sale of alcohol licences were very expensive and customers would take their own wine to drink with their food."

After the wonderful stay in Australia, it was time to head back home via Singapore where it was agreed they would rendezvous with Harry Kar and his wife in Hong Kong. They'd been friends with the Chinese restauranteur from Brigg for many years and they were passing through the city at the same time. Harry had landed first and waited for Francois and Sue at the arrivals gate. In the event, meeting up wasn't that simple, as Francois recalls:

"We came from passport control into the arrivals area and started looking for Harry. With him being Chinese, as a joke, I nicknamed him 'Yellow Swine.' There were hundreds of Chinese people in the area and it was impossible to see Harry in the crowd. So, I hit on the idea of shouting, 'Are you there, yellow swine.' I couldn't hear any answer amongst the hubbub of voices, so I kept shouting it. Suddenly, Harry and his wife appeared out of the blue. He seemed a little concerned as some of the by-standers were turning a bit shirty as they seemed to get the impression that I was calling them yellow swine! We hurried off to avoid a mini-riot! After the airport incident we all met up with our friends Paul and Annie Wilson, who at the time were antique dealers from Hull. The temperature in Hong Kong was exceptionally high. Harry told us not to worry as he'd fixed up a minibus. We all piled inside, but after just a few minutes, I had to get out as I was feeling faint with the intense heat."

In the few days that the party spent in the area, they sampled some of the local delicacies – including dishes with pigeon, frog and snake. Whilst the food was fresh and tasty, there was some revulsion at the exceptionally poor treatment of the animals – especially in a nearby village.

"In the village Market at Mong Kok, we saw things that put us right off. The treatment of animals was disgusting. They skinned snakes alive and cut off the heads of frogs immediately before cooking. After we got back to Hull, Sue couldn't face a Chinese meal for months after that experience."

Mong Kok is described in the Guinness Book of Records as the busiest district anywhere on the planet. In films, it is often portrayed as a seedy area with bars and night clubs run by Triads. Markets specialise in women's clothing, cosmetics and accessories. Restaurants serve different kinds of cuisine and the many food booths serve traditional snacks. These finger foods are apparently very popular for people on the run. Francois and Sue were not on any wanted list – but they were now ready to fly home and it was soon business as usual back in East Yorkshire.

Now retired as head of Catering at Hull City Council, Mike Clayphan recalls working with Francois at Willerby Manor and for a time at Chez Francois in Hull city centre.

"Francois was a great boss and was at his brilliant best with customers. He could be cheeky in a very funny way and play the room. Customer service was his real strength. Yet, although he was fastidious with standards and could be a bit of a pain at times in this respect, he was otherwise really good with his staff. At Willerby Manor, we had a lot of business clients. Occasionally, they would try to show off to their guests by talking down to the waiters as if they were their own minnions. Francois would insist that his team were treated with respect. We knew that he would not tolerate poor behaviour from clients - yet dealt with any transgressions tactfully. On one occasion, a diner had been snapping his fingers and whistling as if the person was his pet dog. Francois went over with a smile, lifted the tablecloth and announced firmly to the table that animals were not allowed in the restaurant. He made the point, but in a way that didn't alienate the customer concerned. I have recounted that tale to many people over the years."

When Derek Baugh eventually left the hotel to take up a new challenge at The Manor House in Walkington, the move was a severe blow to Francois:

"It hit me hard because I was completely happy at the Willerby Manor and working with Derek. I didn't think about working anywhere else. His departure unsettled me."

The event heralded the further rotation of the career wheel for Francois. The spokes were turning and almost inevitably another opportunity came into view.

* * *

Francois was approached by Hull businessman Francis Daly who proposed that he work for him as General Manager at Hesslewood Hall Hotel & Restaurant– on the site of the old Hessle orphanage. It was an offer of an initial three-year contract which he decided to accept. It was a level of responsibility and breadth of control that appealed to him. The challenge proved too attractive to turn down. Historic Hesslewood Hall, sometimes called Hesslewood House, dates-back to the eighteenth century. Coming into the ownership of the Pease family in 1788, the cream brick Grade II listed building was sold in 1920 to provide accommodation for the children of seafarers who had been orphaned. Hitherto, they had been located in a building in Spring Bank, Hull – next to St Jude's church.

Towards the turn of the twentieth century, the building became a hotel and restaurant under the ownership of Hull businessman Francis Daly. Subsequently, it was developed for other commercial purposes. In its time as a hotel and restaurant,

Hesslewood Hall was of a very high standard. It was almost always fully booked thanks in large part to the appointment of a talented chef. Head-hunting Francois to lead the operation was yet another masterstroke by the owner. Not only did he bring in a man with experience and high repute, the talent swoop led to an additional appointment to the kitchen staff in the form of a French commis chef who followed Francois from Willerby Manor. As a bonus, Sue followed her husband, adding her experience to the housekeeping team. Such decisions are never easy. Francois was mindful of the trust and respect that had been afforded him by his previous employers. Whilst a new challenge beckoned, it was not made without a great deal of sadness.

On matters relating to the restaurant menus, Francois wisely consulted with the chef and allowed him to input ideas. He believed this was central to success. The cuisine was French and English – a combination that had worked well in the past at the Willerby Manor. Given his experience and close contact with the customers, Francois was able to input what he believed the customers would like to see on the menu. This enabled wild creativity to be restrained within the boundaries of a marketable list of mouth-watering delights. The ability to divine what would appeal to the customer was a vital contribution to success. The skill required culinary knowledge and importantly a rapport with the client.

Whilst at Hesslewood Hall, Francois bumped into a local councillor in the village. David Ireland was a hard-working local representative and revealed to Francois that he was looking to have Hessle twinned with a European town. Of course, Francois suggested that Bourg-de-Thizy might be a suitable candidate.

Together, the two men worked with the respective councils and succeeded in delivering a twinning arrangement that delivered exchange visits and a sharing of cultural understanding between the two communities. Decades later, the arrangement continues with a Twinning Association overseeing communication and contact between the two towns. The Thizy les Bourgs website contains the following text:

'In 1988, Michel Brondel, mayor of Bourg de Thizy and David Ireland, his English counterpart, with the help of Jean Francois Primpied, restauranteur in England, inaugurated the first exchange between our two municipalities. Since then, alternately, adult exchanges have taken place every year. In 2018, Bourg de Thizy will receive its English friends for the 30th Anniversary from May 21 to 31.'

The Hessle Twinning Association maintains a social media presence to keep members connected through the year.

With wealthy guests staying at the hotel, it was an absolute necessity to ensure that the restaurant's reputation matched that of the establishment. To recruit a leader with all the credentials including impeccable standards in hotel and restaurant management was a sound business decision. Always well-presented with highly polished shoes, the dress code for Francois at Hesslewood Hall was formal. He normally wore either a dinner suit or white tuxedo and black evening dress trousers. Steaks were always a favourite with local clients and business guests at the Hesslewood Hall Hotel itself. As part of his managerial duties, Francois would flambe specialty steaks at the tables and prepare the sauces. The whole exercise entertained diners, not least because of the accompanying charm and wit that was the essence of dining with Francoi at any location.

"In addition to cooking steaks and sauces at the table, I also prepared desserts. One popular sweet was my Mixed Fruit Picasso. It contained fresh fruits - including strawberries, orange segments, pear and peaches. Cointreau or Gran Marnier would then be added."

By promoting the French Menu, Francois allowed free rein to his sense of humour and astute marketing sense. The popular TV comedy programme "Allo Allo" was the inspiration for a theme evening based on that series. Guests turned up dressed-up as characters from the programme.

"We let the smell of garlic waft into the dining area and decorated the place with strings of onions and other French regalia. The guests got into the spirit of it. The chance to get dressed up as Renee the café owner or one of the characters like Herr Flick and come along to eat good food in a jolly atmosphere proved a big draw. People liked hiring the costumes beforehand, getting dressed-up and everything associated with the night out."

Hesslewood Hall was frequented by various TV personalities. Stan Richards, who died in February 2005, played the iconic gamekeeper Seth Armstrong in ITV's soap opera Ennerdale Farm. Whilst visiting Hesslewood Hall, Stan delighted restaurant guests with a demonstration of his musical talents on the piano – to the accompaniment of Francois on the accordion! Stan, as Seth, was no stranger to the instrument – having tinkled on the ivories in an episode at the Woolpack pub. Francois met the late Richard Whitely OBE DL when he came to the Hesslewood Hall hotel and restaurant. In his early career, Richard was a presenter on Yorkshire TV's Calendar where was once bitten live on air by a ferret. From 1998 until his death in 2005, Richard held the honorary title of Mayor of Wetwang – a village in East Yorkshire. As a guest in the same hotel as Margaret Thatcher at the time of the Brighton Bombing, he was immediately on scene to interview the Prime Minister in the chaotic and tragic aftermath of the explosion. The host of various TV shows, he became a much-loved national personality. Francois recalls:

"Richard was a really nice chap. We met several times at the restaurant. He kindly invited me on to the ITV Calendar programme to demonstrate some Christmas dishes but unfortunately it was not possible for me to do it at the time due to other pressures. It was always interesting to meet well-known people and understand what they were like in their everyday lives. I was very impressed by Richard Whitely."

Francis Daly, was naturally keen to exploit any marketing opportunities to promote his business. One scheme designed to gain publicity was centred on the celebration of Beaujolais Nouveau Day which is marked each year in France and in more distant climes on the third Thursday in November. The Beaujolais Nouveau region comprises some 4,000 vineyards producing around a dozen officially-designated types of the cherry-red vintage which is best served chilled and drunk young. In 2017, 27.5 million cases were produced – with 40% being exported. The French organise music, fireworks and festivals to celebrate the day. In the Beaujolais region alone around 120 events are held annually. Being the first to obtain a bottle in the Hull and East Yorkshire area was the perfect project for Francis to gain publicity from what became an annual race.

"So that we could compete in the race to be the first in the area to obtain a bottle of the coveted wine, Francis flew over to France in a light aircraft. He was a determined individual and always up for a challenge. Having secured the precious cargo, he immediately returned and dropped a bottle over Hull in the early hours of the morning.I remember playing the accordion whilst TV crews filmed the drop. The stunt allowed us rightly to claim that we were the first in the region to secure the new Beaujolais. Francis didn't mess around with a parachute for the bottle. It came down packed in a wellington boot!"

The hotel and restaurant operation at Hesslewood Hall relied on teamwork. Francois had the benefit of a brilliant assistant - Terry. Amongst his talents was the ability to perform as a toastmaster at wedding receptions that were held at the hotel. Such gatherings provided an important income for the business. Normally, they were joyous gatherings with everyone in good spirits. However, on one occasion, the event suddenly took on a more sinister tone as there was a disagreement amongst the two families.

"Terry was a fantastic assistant-manager and I had every confidence in him. I had taken the day off and left him to take full charge of the wedding reception. Suddenly, it all kicked-off with the two families falling-out. They became angry and started throwing food at each other. Trying to be the peacemaker, Terry got caught in the crossfire and despite being someone not to be trifled with, ended up getting hit in the face with a pudding! After a while it calmed down - but not before he ended up wearing most of the dessert course."

Whilst at Hesslewood Hall, Francois invited his old friend Franco Ciuffatelli to look around. By this time his former boss had established his own successful business at the Millhouse Restaurant on the outskirts of Skidby. The pair shared a sense of humour and inevitably the visit included a demonstration of one of the hotel's most unusual beds.

"We took Franco to one of the bedrooms and invited him to hop on to the water bed that Francis had decided to install for the more adventurous guests. He'd had never seen one before, let alone tried to sleep on one. He confidently jumped on to the bed and we just fell about laughing as his small rotund shape bounced around uncontrollably. He was trapped in a constant wobble and the more he tried to get off, the worse it got. In the end, we had to wrestle him upright and on to solid ground! We were all crying with laughter."

Running any hotel always involves hard work and a degree of stress, but unpredictable events always helped ensure that boredom was never a problem. Hesslewood Hall had formerly been a children's orphanage. It was reputed to have a ghost. Tales of past supernatural events abounded and one day such an event occurred whilst Francois was on duty.

"I was in my office, when a white-faced porter suddenly burst into the room. He dragged me along to the function room toilet. The area was not open to the public at the time, so it should have been empty. One of the two cubicles was locked from the inside. I climbed up and it was empty, but I felt a cold shiver. As we walked away down the corridor, we heard a bang from the room. When we returned, the toilet door was now wide open and we could hear the laughter of children. The porter, who had armed himself with a brush handle, was shitting himself. We agreed, that calling the police was not an option. After that, he refused to go anywhere near the toilets.

"There were other happenings. One Christmas, Sue and I stayed in the hotel annex. We were the only ones sleeping there. We had prepared 40 champagne glasses as a Christmas Day drink for the folks in the next-door nursing home. The glasses had been left upside down. After taking the dog for a walk, we locked up - with only us in the building. During the night the dog started whining, but refused to go forward when we opened our bedroom door. The next morning, before anyone had arrived, we went downstairs only to find that there were only three glasses left on the table. Later, we had an Aussie rugby player staying at the hotel. One morning he asked me if we had ghosts. He said that he had heard laughing in the night and in the morning found his window open and papers all over the floor. He claimed that he had closed the window before going to sleep."

Although unpredictable things happened, life at the hotel had a rhythm to it. At the rear, leading to the river, was a large area of grassland with a few trees dotted here and there. At 5pm every day, four peacocks would parade in a line past the hotel and walk towards one of the trees. They would then ascend into the branches and make a bed high up for the night. The birds were colourful and elegant, adding style and poise to the grounds. To provide balance, the hotel owner decided to buy an Irish Cockerel.

"The cockerel was a nasty little shit. It used to run after us and bite us in the leg. It had seen the daily ritual of the peacocks but could not reach the branches. Francis decided to give it a helping hand and placed a long plank up against the tree. This was enough to enable it to get in amongst the peacocks. They were not happy, as the cockerel would try and fight its way to a better spot. One day we noticed that a peacock had tail feathers missing but we suspected that this had been caused by a fox."

There is no shortage of animal anecdotes from the Hesslwood Hall days. One of the gardeners at the hotel owned a rottweiler which accompanied him at times when he was at work. The animal had a very friendly nature and Francois was happy for it to come into his office for a snooze. One day, the dog was sitting calmly looking at Francois as he sat at his desk. As the minutes ticked, by the dog's gaze became more fixed.

"I was calmly sitting there working and noticed the dog looking at me. Over the space of just a few minutes, I sensed a change in the atmosphere. The dog's eyes were fixed on me in a sort of stare. It began growling and salivating. I felt sure it was ready to attack. Luckily, the owner had heard and took control of the animal."

It seems there are many reasons why a dog might stare at a human. It can be a sign of affection or a means of gaining attention – especially if it feels that food might be shared. It might not always be a good idea to stare back at the animal – as this can be interpreted as rudeness - or even a threat. Salivation is hard-wired into a dog – with food being the unconditioned stimulus! It is also the case, that dogs can drool when stressed. Looking back, although the incident would unnerve anyone, its seems to have been a simple misunderstanding between Francois and the Rottweiller! There was one more animal tale that is funny - but only after the event. Hesslewood Hall was extremely popular as a wedding destination. The grounds provided multiple opportunities for photographers to shoot great images. On every wedding photographer's must-do list is the classic "cake shot" featuring the bride and groom making the first cut. All arrangements were in place and the magnificent and very expensive wedding cake had already been delivered the day before the event. It was placed on the immaculately laid-out table ready on the next day for the entire wedding party to admire and eat. Unfortunately, an external door leading out on to the rolling grounds beyond had been left open to let in fresh air on what was a warm afternoon. Unfortunately, fresh air was not the only thing that had entered the room.

"We went in last thing on the afternoon before the wedding day to check that everything was ok and ready for the guests the next day. To our horror, we saw that a goat had wandered in and was busy scoffing the wedding cake. We chased the animal out and looked in horror at the cake which had a large chunk missing. We ran to find the pastry chef but he had already gone home. Luckily, we had time to fix the problem! Talk about feeling more than a little sheepish the next day."

Frances Daly had various other business interests – including the Waterfront nightclub in Hull
which had been opened circa 1979. During the
filming of a "Fools and Horses" special in the city,
Derek Edward Trotter (Del Boy) played by David
Jason and Rodney Charlton Trotter (Rodders)
played by Nicholas Lyndhurst were staying at the
Waterfront Hotel. It was a no-brainer for the pair
to dine at the Heslewood Hall restaurant. Whilst
they were not yet Millionaires, Francois was delighted to welcome them - although the chan-
deliers were declared out of bounds for reasons
known only to devotees of the sit-com. At the end
of the evening, Francois gave the dodgy traders a
lift back to the Waterfront. He was generously rewarded with a gift of thirty 405-line black and
white "rare vintage" TVs. Also, for just forty quid
he was offered and refused a stock clearance of
cute dolls that sang "My Way" by Frank Sinatra in
Japanese. In parting, whilst puffing a cigar on the
kerb, Del declared, Bonjour Francois!" In his rear
view mirror, Francois saw the pair leg-it at the appearance of two constables.

Having served for three years at the Hesslewood
Hall, Francois was happy in his work. It was a
great restaurant with brilliant staff – and he had an
excellent relationship with the owner. Aside from
dipping his toes in the water of owning his own
place after his period at the Royal Station Hotel,
there had since been no opportunity to launch out

meaningfully in his own right. When he was approached by highly successful local businessman Eddie Healey, Francois found himself attracted by a quite unique offer to run his own show.

TO MEADOWHALL
& BACK

A self-made millionaire, the late Eddie Healey and his brother Malcolm started their road to success when working together in their father's corner shop. Eddie eventually branched out into property and partnered with Paul Sykes to develop a derelict site on the outskirts of Sheffield upon which rose the Meadowhall Shopping Centre. This was eventually sold to British Land for a reported £1.17 Billion. Eddie approached Francois at a time just prior to the Meadowhall opening. It was still technically a building site and his suggestion was for Francois take a unit in the shopping centre where it was envisaged shoppers would be offered a wide variety of choice in terms of cuisine. It was thought that a French café would provide variety and help attract visitors to the centre. With personal experience of how Francois operated, Eddie, or 'Mr Meadowhall' as he was later described in the written press, had identified Francois as the perfect fit.

"I went along to Sheffield and visited the almost complete new shopping centre with Eddie. We looked around, dressed in all the safety gear, as is compulsory on a live building site. It was sensational. A simply massive development. I hadn't seen anything like it before on that scale. I was in awe. Eddie proposed that I take a unit in the Oasis area right next to the cinema. It wasn't cheap, but he undertook to do all the fitting out and decorations. In every sense, it was a real challenge and an exciting business opportunity."

Francois had reached a point where he had gained considerable experience in hotels and restaurant management. Although he was a capable chef in his own right with a clear work ethic and impeccable standards, he also had a natural and powerful rapport with customers. It was his forte. It was combination of sharp wit, French charm and a generally friendly approach. In a café setting, the latter attributes were vital ingredients. This would certainly be noted as a strength in any business plan. In financial terms, every new business launch carries some financial risk. The Meadowhall opportunity offered the prospect of extensive footfall. To achieve profit though, the prospective café's menu offering to its customers needed to be in line with what a passing shoppers might require – and at a price they would be willing to pay. It was obvious to Francois that whatever appeared on the menu, margins would be tight. Although the chance to operate his own business in a scintillating, busy and innovative environment was extremely tempting, the calculus on whether to proceed ultimately rested on the matter of financial risk. The question of whether to take a chance was hung in a precarious balance.

In the end, the answer was to be found in spreading the financial exposure by taking on a trusted financial partner. It was best friend Jacques Meilhan who threw his hat into the ring and took on joint shareholding of Café Francois at Meadowhall. The enterprise was a roaring success. At its peak, the business served up to 2000 clients per week. Meadowhall attracted thousands of regular customers from near and far. Folk liked the experience and returned time and again. Footfall was key for the business to succeed. With such a high turnover of customers, Francois needed the considerable support of wife Sue who grasped the challenge with both hands – effectively sharing the role of greeting and serving clients and helping manage the enterprise. Francois fully acknowledges her part in his business success:

"Sue's contribution was immense along with son Philip who became part of the service team. Jacques Meilhan became a shareholder and helped in many ways. His wife Lynne managed our books. It was a big team effort that worked really well."

Jacques, has great recollections of the Meadowhall project.

"I helped with maintenance work as and when required. On rare occasions I'd help serve customers. It was a very busy café and great fun. I sometimes went over on Saturdays to lend a hand. On offer was a range of coffees, pies, sandwiches and cakes. It amused me that there was always a really good stock of a special ice cream brand which Francois really loved. I got the impression he didn't want to sell it to the customers and would rather eat it all himself!"

In fact, the ice cream was special. It was the Movenpick brand which was of Swiss origin and produced by Nestle. Initially, the ice cream was only available in selected restaurants and it wasn't until 2002 that the product was licensed for distribution in the United Kingdom. Looking back, Francois recalls his addiction:

"I did love that ice cream and I did have too much of it. True. But we did sell some to the customers! If only I'd had less, I might not have had the health problems I have today!"

Francois at Meadowhall was a café and not a restaurant. It sold hot and cold drinks and basic snacks. The business was successful and there was that important contact with people. Again, Francois was in his element. He wanted to please people. Easy, free, on-site parking, extensive covered shopping malls and a relaxing experience trumped the city shopping streets where congested roads, aggressive parking regimes and the vagaries of the weather all conspired to swing the balance in favour of the new concept in retail. At Meadowhall, the variety of eateries in the Oasis area was stunning – and not all were fast-food. As the months went by, the satisfaction of banking the proceeds of a thriving business were tempered by excessive workloads. Francois began to feel the strain intensely. There was constant pressure of work and daily travel to and from home – a two-hour round trip which covered 130 miles per day. Sleep was at a premium. Despite the café being successful, there was a price to pay. It sapped his energy - but not his determination:

"Café Francois was a hit with the public from the start. Everything about the operation worked like clockwork and we made money. The problem was that I had to commute daily. It gradually made me very tired and stressed. The enjoyment started to fade and I began to wonder whether it was time to develop something nearer to home. I was getting only about five hours sleep and it became clear to me that I couldn't sustain the pace for much longer. Things needed to change."

Right on cue, but without knowing that he would be pushing at an open door, Willerby Manor boss John Townend went to see Francois at Meadowhall. He made what Francois felt was the right opportunity at exactly the right time. Although the business at Meadowhall continued for a further 8 months under son Stephen's stewardship, Francois and Sue would no longer make the daily trek to Sheffield

✱ ✱ ✱

The Willerby Manor Hotel had been a happy hunting ground for Francois. He'd loved his previous 15-year stint and had got on very well with the owner and senior management. Now he was to be the main man under the overall direction of the owners. Formerly an accountant, John Townend (1934-2018) had served in the Royal Air Force as a commissioned Pilot Officer. Subsequently, he joined The House of Townend – a Hull wine merchant and 1979, became the Member of Parliament for Bridlington - retiring in 2001.

"John Townend offered me the job as General Manager at Willerby Manor. As I understood, his company owned the hotel. I had full day to day control of the hotel and restaurant operations. My previous long stint there had been a great experience. It was a role I had always wanted. Although running my own business had a certain appeal, the daily commute to Sheffield was not viable in personal health terms. I opted to take the job. I was back in Willerby and just a few minutes from home."

As General Manager at Willerby Manor, Francois assumed almost the same role as Derek Baugh had done in the earlier time at the hotel. Companies House records show that Francois was a director at the Willerby Manor between 27 October 1991 and 1 December 1991. The Hotel, which is conveniently located in the western suburbs of Hull, attracted visitors to the city because of its reputation for fine food and excellent accommodation. On his return, Francois was delighted to see that Bob Steele, Head Chef for Events, was still on the payroll. Bob was much respected by Francois for his cooking skills, long service, unswerving loyalty and terrific work ethic. In his senior role, Francois was no stranger to dealing with guests with big reputations. In some cases they had even bigger egos:

"A famous Yorkshire batsman once stayed at the hotel. It had been snowing heavily and he seemed to expect someone at the hotel to remove the snow from his car. Whilst I always try to please guests, I did not feel that it was reasonable to ask a member of staff to carry out a task they were not contracted to do. If we had done it for him, then in fairness we would have to do it for all the guests. My polite refusal did not go down well with the individual concerned. In contrast, some years earlier, the late Yorkshire and England fast bowler Freddie Trueman had stayed with us. He was a lovely, genuine man. I found him very pleasant, respectful and down to earth. It was an honour to meet him."

Taking a short break that year Francois and Sue travelled to Paris on holiday. They visited Monmartre - close to the Basilica of the Sacred Heart – the city's second most popular tourist destination. In the evening, at 8pm, they chose to dine at a 2 Star Michelin restaurant. They went along with friends in a party of eight. The group enjoyed their starters and the service was in keeping with the reputation of a Michelin starred establishment. In France, diners usually took their time over food, taking the opportunity to chat at length through an evening at the restaurant. When the main course arrived immediately after the starter plates had been cleared, alarm bells started to ring.

"I asked the waiter why the main course had arrived so quickly. He explained that the working time rules had changed in France. New legislation affected the length of the working week and impacted on pay. As a result, the owners couldn't afford to have the level of chef cover as before. Overtime was banned and opening times were being squeezed. Some items on the menu that in the past had been cooked personally by the chef as ordered were now prepped by him and cooked by others, when required."

Some time later, Francois was reading a French paper and saw that the owner of the restaurant had died of a heart attack. Although it isn't possible to attribute this to any specific cause, he felt sure that the pressures of maintaining the two-star Michelin standards when employment laws were being tightened would not have helped the man's health. It was something to bear in mind when reviewing his own situation. Later, when taking a short break in the village of Oppede Le Vieux in France, Francois encountered what can only be described as a quite bizarre coincidence.

As was his routine, he'd strolled into a local newsagent to collect his usual copy of the Sunday Telegraph. What happened next defied belief. The shopkeeper informed Francois that an English gentleman had arrived earlier and bought the last copy of the paper. He described him as looking a bit like the famous French singer Charles Aznavour. Francois was puzzled. His life was full of coincidences and chance meetings with stars – but had the singer really purchased a copy of an English newspaper? That evening, Francois and Sue went to a local restaurant. As they perused the menu, they heard English voices nearby. On glancing in the direction of a chatting couple, Sue said to Francois. "I think I have found your Charles Aznavour. It's your boss John Townend. He's got your paper!" Francois laughed in disbelief:

"I just couldn't believe it. It was pure coincidence. Neither of us had any idea we were going to be on holiday on the same French Village. I got on very well with Mr Townend."

At first, everything at the hotel was just fine. The essentially organisational role presented him with no difficulties. He loved the responsibility as well as working with the team across the organisation. However, after six months, things changed significantly. The owners brought in a junior family member into a senior role alongside Francois. He was not critical about this development or the sincerity and potential of the family member. The move was understandable and in the long-term interests of the individual. However, from a personal point of view, he did not feel that he was able to exert the breadth and degree of control that he felt was in line with the role he had accepted. He was not at all happy and contemplated a move. As if with perfect timing in a time of flux, Francois was approached by the late Jack Brignall, - then a key player with Wykeland who were heavily involved in the new Willerby Shopping Park development less than a mile from the Willerby Manor. He approached Francois in the hope that he would be interested in taking one of the new units.

❋ ❋ ❋

Willerby Shopping Park was developed on newly vacant land following the closure of Willerby Railway Station and the eventual termination of the Hull and Barnsley line in 1964. The new shopping precinct to the west of the Willerby village included a huge car park to service a major supermarket and multiple shop units of varying size – including a DIY centre. When he was shown round, Francois immediately saw something that appealed to him. However, the work that was needed to realise his vision seemed beyond his means at that time.

"When I looked inside the shell of the unit, I had an idea how it could look. In my mind's eye,

I saw it all - the kitchen, the tables, the seating and the overall look. Unfortunately, I just did not have the funds available to complete such works. When I shared my thoughts with Jack Brignall, he did not hesitate to allay my concerns. He simply told me to commit my thoughts to paper and then he would deliver my vision. There was a process to go through with the company. I was invited to discuss the project with senior people at the Wyke-land company. I knew most of them as customers from Willerby Manor. During the meeting, there was an awkward character who I didn't know who kept on asking irritating questions. In the end, I had to remind him that I had not come to attend an interview with him. I told the chap point blank that if I decided to move my business there, it would remain my business. I would be a tenant free from interference in all matters other than the rental agreement. He was sharply put in his place by his colleagues. I had made my name at Willerby Manor and felt I deserved more respect. However, the chance to have my own restaurant again was irresistible. It was very close to my home so there was no issue of travelling time. I decided to take on the challenge. There was no capital cost to me. I'm not sure if setting up the unit to be a restaurant was recouped in the rent - but the overheads were affordable and not a problem in those early years. Jack made it all possible, just as Eddie Healey had done at Meadowhall. They were brilliant."

'Francois' at Willerby Shopping Park had 80

covers and was busy from the first week of opening. Its success just grew and grew. Popular with corporate customers, the restaurant was also held in high esteem by local folk with modest disposable incomes. The character of the restaurant was determined not just by the French and English dishes on the menu, but by the strong French decorative influence and background music. Unsurprisingly, central to the restaurant's ethos was quality in every department. It was a continuing theme throughout Francois' career. Strict cleanliness and good food hygiene were paramount. To reassure customers, the kitchen was designed to be open plan so that clients could see how their food was being prepared and cooked. Sue continued to offer her tangible support and considerable organisational skills. Francois, as ever, was appreciative of her role in the success being experienced:

"Sue and I worked it together. On the balance of time, I spent more in the kitchen, but I always kept in close contact with the clients. Sue was my lieutenant. She spent most of the time at the front of house, generally managing operations, helping take orders and supervising staff."

Opening night at the Willerby Shopping Park comprised invited guests only. Jack Brignall was the guest of honour in recognition of his part in bringing us there. He was then invited every year to continue this recognition.

"At lunchtimes, we offered a café experience to shoppers and anyone who cared to come especially. There was a huge car park to service all the shops. At 5pm we would revert to a restaurant configuration. We designated Friday and Saturday nights as music nights when we brought in entertainment for the diners. We were always busy. On Friday's and Saturdays, we were always packed. December dining was booked almost a year in advance with deposits securing the places."

New Year's Eve was also a major annual event at the restaurant. The celebrations started with a four-course meal and cabaret – usually with a singer or comedian. After Big Ben chimed in the new year at midnight, guests would disco until 2am with cheeses and fruits on hand for those still with an appetite! For anyone with the stamina after that time, Francois would ensure supplies of French onion soup – with some revellers still trickling away at 5 or 6 am.

Francois at Willerby Shopping Park
December 1993

One day, the restaurant was hosting a birthday party. There were many guests. The clients had even hired a pianist to liven up the event. His background music performance went down so well that Francois approached him with an offer to play at the restaurant on Friday and Saturday nights. His act was then augmented by Francois himself on the accordion – plus waiter Fred Harrison on bass. They came together as one act after all the meals were all served.

"Fred had previous experience playing with the extremely popular Norman Mail Band at Grange Park Hotel. He had a terrific sense of humour and talent as a comic. We worked well together and gave the diners a show later in the evening. After a while we introduced a sort of spoof element to the proceedings. We would dress up as famous people and play tunes wearing their respective masks –

usually after 10pm when people had finished their meals. One evening, we began playing 'O Sole Mio.' Fred had gone out the back way and then entered the restaurant from the car park at the front singing the lyrics dressed as Luciano Pavarotti. He'd changed in secret. Fattened-up using cushions, he really looked the part. He certainly got quite close with the voice! On another occasion, I was playing Hava Nagila on the accordion as an intro for Fred to come in dressed as Saddam Hussein with a bazooka. Shortly after Nicho burst in dressed as Bill Clinton. He pulled out a starting pistol and fired blanks at Saddam. The guests loved it! I was crying with laughter. Fred also did a superb Michael Jackson impersonation – including the moon walk. We varied the performance and Nicho our waiter came in one evening from outside dressed as a monkey. Fred went across and took him by the hand before guiding him into the back. Nicho's walk was perfectly rehearsed and gave a very convincing display. These stunts entertained people and word quickly spread."

There was never any trouble at the restaurant. However, police did find it necessary to attend late one evening to check the story of a gentlemen who claimed he was an employee. It was Fred. He'd left for home after his shift still dressed as an Arab Sheikh. Whilst this may have been enough to have attracted the attention of the two patrolling constables, their decision to stop him was rooted in the provisions of the Road Traffic act – rather than some concern about sartorial taste. For reasons best known to himself, Fred had circumnavigated the roundabout in an anticlockwise direction, thus raising suspicions regarding possible excessive alcohol consumption. Such concerns were eventually allayed, but in the meantime, Francois was happy to confirm that Fred was indeed one of the team.

The restaurant was but a short drive from many of the west Hull villages where professionals of all description would spend their retirement years enjoying the good things that life had to offer. One such client was an absent-minded chap in his nineties who seemed a bit like Mr Grace in the series "Are You Being Served." He dined at the restaurant every day and began every meal with a glass of port. The formula at the restaurant worked a treat and the place was packed night after night. At the centre of that success was the quality of the food and the type of menu on offer.

"Wherever I have worked, we always sourced fresh seasonal ingredients of the highest quality available. At Francois in Willerby Shopping Park, we bought our meat from the late Tim May in Cottingham. He delivered at any time we wanted. We did a great deal of business with him. He used to joke that he'd just been to my house. What he meant was that he'd come from home – a property that he'd been able to but thanks to profits of his business with me! It was a bit like the police during the miner's strike. Many officers bought "Scargill" cars thanks to their overtime in that period. Dennis Butler was another great local supplier who provided our fruit and vegetables. French onion soup was a feature on our menu along with frog's legs which were very popular. We made all our own sauces."

Amongst the well-known guests at the Willerby Shopping Park restaurant, Francois found favour with Geoffrey Dickens MP who was so enamoured with the fayre that he went along two nights running whilst on a visit to Hull University. A former polio victim who became a heavyweight boxer, he had been victorious in forty out of sixty fights. During a press conference, he admitted to an affair and stated that he would be leaving his wife. He then asked the media to keep it quiet until he had told her. Dickens was in favour of hanging. It was easy to suppose that having heard of his infidelity, his wife would have been keen to see him swinging on the gallows – but in fact two weeks after the announcement they were reconciled. His satisfaction with the food and service provided by Francois and Sue were relayed in an extremely complimentary letter sent on House of Commons notepaper in which he noted that he and his wife had thoroughly enjoyed their meals.

Perhaps one of the most bizarre incidents encountered at the Willerby Shopping Park restaurant involved a regular guest who had brought his family along to enjoy an evening out. They had completed their meal and were preparing to leave after having settled the bill. The restaurant's toilets were situated at the back of the unit and the passageway leading to it was used to hang coats. Little suspicion was raised when the male adult guest went to the toilet. However, some minutes later, when he reappeared wearing his overcoat, staff were somewhat startled to see that he appeared to have suddenly gained a huge amount of weight.

"My wife Sue brought my attention to the almost bizarre sight. Seconds after he had gone out of the door, we realised that two cushions were missing from some spare seats that were kept in the corridor. We immediately went outside and found the man sitting at the wheel of his extremely expensive car. I asked him if he had forgotten anything, but at first he tried to remain puzzled - a picture of innocence. When I mentioned the missing cushions, he became angry and threatened to sue me at the very suggestion it could have been him. When he realised that I had witnesses, he admitted the theft and produced the missing cushions. He told me that his wife had taken a fancy to them and he was merely trying to please her. It wasn't a matter of the money. He had millions. Whilst the man may not have seen removing the cushions as a criminal act, it was theft – pure and simple. If he'd shown honesty and respect by offering to buy them, instead of simply taking them without permission, we would have considered his request. Had we contacted the police, his reputation would have been in tatters. It was a foolish act, perhaps on the spur of the moment – but nevertheless a lesson to him, I hoped."

Another disappointment came when a former member of staff at the restaurant also committed a criminal act. It was rare for Francois to have to dismiss anyone. However, he compromised little when it came to standards of service and for that reason eventually had to dispense with the services of a waiter.

"One evening I went out of the back door to enjoy a cigar before finally closing for the night. My car was parked nearby. I noticed that the paintwork seemed to be different. When I inspected the bodywork more closely, I found that it was covered in acid burns. When we checked the security cameras, I found that it had been a former member of staff who had taken revenge on my car. Whilst the insurance claim resulted in my being provided with a new vehicle, it was nevertheless very disappointing to discover his bitter reaction to being dismissed."

Each Christmas, Francois organised a staff party at the restaurant. Some customers and suppliers were also invited. It was usually a very popular event, but one year, Francois noticed that one of his team was attracting particular attention.

"I was bemused at first. I saw a crowd of guests

surrounding one of my staff. It was like a rugby scrum. When I went to see what was happening, a young waitress was trying to sell dope to my butcher. He was telling her that he was already crazy and needed no further help from her! She was trying to make money on the side and looked completely stoned to me. I don't tolerate drugs. I drove her home and took the decision to dispense with her services. It was the last time we ran such an event. However, one of my pals Alan Dixon ran the Newland Park Hotel & Tudor House. We decided to do a joint staff party at the Newland Park. When I say joint, I mean a combined event!"

On a more pleasant note, the occasion of a milestone birthday for wife Sue, inspired Francois to arrange for some special celebrities to attend her birthday party at the restaurant. Invited guests, including family and friends, witnessed the sensational surprise appearance of the Bootleg Beatles band on the eve of their opening at the Millennium Stadium. The group's fee, normally an eye-watering sum, had been dramatically cut as a personal gesture to Francois as he was someone they had known from their earlier days whilst doing gigs at the Willerby Manor Hotel. Francois recalls:

"I had their number from the Willerby Manor days. They agreed straight away to come for Sue's party. At the time they were performing in Scotland and were about to continue their tour into Wales. We were not too much of a detour on their way there, so it worked out perfectly. Sue was over the moon and everyone had a fantastic evening."

Francois had paid a fitting tribute to his wife, who had been by his side over the years and in various roles had given her all to the cause. Sue would not have ideally chosen a life in catering and it was to her credit that she supported her husband without fail. Yet there were times when her patience wore thin with some clients. She did not suffer fools gladly and on occasion this caused blips in the trend of largely five-star comments the restaurant enjoyed on review sites. One contributor went as far as to suggest that she "should not be in catering." Sue is the first to admit that she struggled at times to remain civil with some customers. It was all part of the mix – and most clients found it irresistible. Although always amiable and keen to please his clients, Francois had some red lines he would not allow people to cross. When it came to discounts or freebies for customers, these were always at his discretion. All establishments have a responsibility to be run at a profit to avoid financial issues – a problem seen all too often during hard times. An "amuse bouche" was often provided as an appetiser 'on the house.' Such considerations were not too costly for the restaurant to produce - and in any event provided value to the restaurant as a goodwill gesture. However, when it came to requests from customers for a free bottle of wine or a free drink, then the economics became more problematic. Francois had a strict policy on srequestes for freebies:

"Occasionally, customers would ask if I would provide a free bottle of wine or concession as it was their birthday - or for some other reason. I always politely informed them that our prices did not allow for this and if I did it for one person, it was only fair that it was available to all. The only way to make this work would be to add it to the general prices. It is true that occasionally I would make an exception but when that happened, it would do it by my heart - and not because somebody asked for it. I found that these requests were becoming more and more frequent."

Francois and Sue made a point of taking holidays in set weeks of the year to enable them to travel to France. It was on one of these trips that the couple travelled on the Eurostar train. The train had been travelling for some minutes when eagle-eyed Sue fastened her gaze on a man sitting next to Francois. In as discrete manner as she could, she whispered to Francois – "Look who is sitting next to you." Turning his head to the right casually as if glance towards the opposite window, Francois immediately recognised the man was none other than guitarist Bill Wyman of Rolling Stones fame. The bass player had left the Stones in 1993 and eventually toured with The Rhythm Kings. A musician himself, Francois had no hesitation in opening a conversation:

"Bill Wyman was totally relaxed and down to

earth. He was on his way to play in a concert in Nice. We talked throughout the journey. He spoke more than I did. By coincidence, he knew some of the musicians I had played with as a youngster. One of the guys was called Monty of Sens Unique. Unfortunately, he had died. I had been on stage with him with the backing band. Unfortunately, we couldn't take up Bill's invitation to attend his concert because we were on our way to Provence."

During his time at the Willerby Shopping Park, Francois had taken on the role as Chairman of the East Riding Restaurant Association. The Vice Chairman was Derek Baugh, his former boss. The organisation's treasurer was Paul Wyman of Tickton Grange and the secretary George Tambaros of The Omellete. The organisation was twinned with Cote D'Opale Restaurant Association in Calais. This arrangement was a great opportunity to travel to France with wives for a few days of relaxation and networking. Calais was also a regular stopover for Francois and Sue on their way to holidays in the south. They were familiar with the area, had restauranteurs as friends and the lines of communication were to prove very useful.

Although everything in the Willerby Shopping Park garden seemed rosy, there were some unsettling influences being brought to bear. Whilst the rents over the previous 15 years had remained affordable under the Wykeland stewardship of the site, changes under a new regime were starting to cause concern. The unit had attracted the interest of a banking group who wanted to establish a presence in the area. It was a trend seen elsewhere. The high street was becoming a hunting ground for building societies and other financial institutions. Small family concerns were being squeezed-out by large retail companies and supermarket chains. With rents rising significantly, Francois was approached by a multinational banking group who wanted to open an office in the shopping park. Facing unaffordable rents, but reluctant to uproot what was an extremely successful business, he carefully considered his options. As he pondered a lucrative offer from Santander, an opportunity arose in Northern France where a friend was closing his restaurant business at Guines which was located close to the Eurotunnel terminal.

"I found myself torn between staying in Willerby or relocating to a new challenge in France. My existing business was successful, but the rent was set to rise significantly. I had received a tempting financial offer to quit the unit. It was unsettling. After long consideration, Sue and I decided to move the business to France. However, I had made my home in Willerby and I was happy in the area where we had made many friends. So, the plan was to stay in France for just three years and then come back. In any case, I didn't see myself living in my home country – especially in the north where I had seen a lot of anti-British feeling."

The journey across the channel represented the start of a new venture but there was clarity that the move was temporary. Yet there was a feeling of freshness and challenge about the immediate future. It was a change - and perhaps also as good as a rest.

ALLO ALLO

S ailing across the Channel to France to start a new phase in his restaurant career gave Francois some food for thought. Had he not, but a few years earlier, travelled in the opposite direction? On that journey, he had not pondered too deeply about the possible unintended conse- quences of his journey. The prospect of being away from family and friends had caused some feelings of unease. Now, having made his home in East Yorkshire, he was travelling back to France for what had been mapped-out as a three-year exped- ition. Would this become a permanent posting? He would certainly miss the friends he had made in East Yorkshire. Yet the spot near Calais meant easy access to relatives in the South - and trips back across the Channel were not that daunting.

The ferry journey was uneventful and the route not quite as breath-taking as the one undertaken by another Francois in history. On 7 January 1785, Jean-Pierre-Francois Blanchard and Dr John Jeffries left Dover in a hydrogen-filled balloon. It was a clear and calm day as they drifted across the channel. Some two and a half hours later they landed close to Guines in the Pas-de-Calais. To maintain height the pair had to jettison their equipment – and most of their clothing. At least Francois would arrive in Guines wearing his trousers and a casual shirt. The daring balloon flight is captured in an oil painting on canvas. It now hangs in the London Science Museum. Francois and Sue did not trouble to record their trip in oils – mainly because theirs had not been the first such journey by ferry! To historians, any mention of Guines will almost certainly trigger tales of medieval sieges and the appraisal of ancient military tactics to conquer a French enemy – including bribery! The Castle of Guines was six miles south of English-held Calais and an important link for the French defences. In 1832, English prisoners of war were detained in the fortifications. They were freed by an escapee who returned at night with a group of men. Together, they took over the castle. French emissaries were sent to London to plead with Edward III to order his men out. Whilst denying any knowledge of the raid, he initially agreed to provide a note asking for anyone in the castle to return it to the rightful owner. Shortly afterwards, after taking some stick from parliamentarians, he changed his mind and sent troops to reinforce the existing garrison. After laying siege to the castle, a 4500-strong French attacking force were humiliated by a mere 115 defenders. It led to the French giving up on the castle.

When Francois rolled into town some centuries later, locals bore no historical bad blood towards a fellow Frenchman setting up shop in the town.

The new enterprise at Guines in the Calais region was situated in tranquil grounds which contained a farmhouse and an 18th century moated manor house – known as 'The Castle.'   No - not that castle - but close! Francois had decided to rent the farmhouse for a period of three years. He called his new restaurant La Ferme Gourmande (The Gourmet's Farm). At the same time, he and Sue bought a house in a small village nearby. Things fell into place pretty-smoothly. There was a fresh feeling of excitement in setting up a new business. It was all full of promise and there was a hustle-bustle from employing new staff and looking forward to meeting new clients. The substantial premises comprised a restaurant and seven bedrooms. Guests included diners from the local area. To them, there was hardly a novelty in having a French chef. They were French themselves and knew what to expect in a French restaurant. Their imperative, with the cuisine as a given, was price. And no matter how little they paid for the meal, first class, five star, finger-snapping attentiveness was something that most expected. And they expected it all night long.

Happily, diners included clients who had previously frequented the Willerby restaurant. Some called-in whilst on motoring or coaching holidays in Europe. Others came especially on a pilgrimage to taste the food and renew old friendships. Yet others, arrived for the first time and one of those brought with her some unusual co-diners. At first, the arrival of two very impressive motorhomes in the car park, drew only minimal attention. The visitors had booked in advance under what turned out to be false names. As the party approached the doorway, their demeanour signalled that this was no ordinary restaurant booking and the visitors were not Jacques and Josephine public. Walking towards the restaurant was the British Labour foreign secretary, her husband - and covertly armed police bodyguards. They were no strangers to a square meal and would have not looked out of place on the pitch at The Boulevard. In typical British style, they were the epitome of politeness. More than that, leaving aside the menu, some of their number had already checked-out the restaurant for possible threats. Francois and his team did not feel intimidated by the high security and over several subsequent visits came to enjoy the presence of their high-profile guests.

"Margaret Beckett was such a pleasant lady. Her protection detail always thoroughly checked the place before she entered. They used to camp nearby and often came to eat at the restaurant. They dined with us one Saturday and stayed for the music afterwards. We had a bass-player, a drummer and I played the accordion and she would happily sing along in tune with her bodyguards to well-known English and French tunes. One of the policemen closest to her always carried a briefcase and I was curious what it contained. My curiosity got the better of me and I finally discovered its secret. Straight out of a James Bond movie, I was told that on the press of a button the case opened out into a bulletproof screen. Thankfully, this explanation was never tested."

Since the restaurant was in a farming area, the food on offer reflected the taste of local clients. Rabbit, pigeon, partridge and wild-bore featured strongly on its menu. Whilst Francois ran the kitchen, Sue supervised the service and practised her French language skills front of house at the tables. Despite the local influence, English and American business clients were regular diners and guests at the hotel.

❋ ❋ ❋

Soon after arriving at Guines, Francois found himself facing what he felt was an over-zealous French policeman – seemingly with a chip on his shoulder. Close to the restaurant was a roundabout which had been chosen by the local police as a suitable focus for their anti-drink driving campaign. On three occasions in the space of four days he had been stopped by the same cop – convinced that his employment at the restaurant rendered him a prime suspect for a drink-driving offence. Francois fully understood that drinking any alcohol whilst driving was frowned on in France. In fact, he only drank lightly on his day off but never drove at all on that day. At the first stop, finding out from the driving licence that it was Francois' birthday the following day, the officer smiled smugly noting that close attention would be given on that day. He hadn't been joking but the subsequent birthday check did not reveal the presence of any alcohol. Feeling that he was being victimised, Francois finally raised his concerns when the officer pulled him in again on the next day.

"On the third stop in as many days, I was fed up of taking the roadside test repeatedly. I'd had enough. It seemed excessive. There was no smell of alcohol on my breath. I told the Gendarme that I wasn't having it. He seemed somewhat amused and chose to wind me up still further by admitting that his suspicions were raised – simply because I worked in the restaurant. He was convinced that meant I routinely drank alcohol."

Local Gendarmes were customers at the restaurant and seemed to Francois to be pleasant characters. However, the official policy appeared to be that police were normally deployed outside the immediate area in which they lived. The overly keen cop was from Boulogne. About a week after the three previous stops, Francois saw the same gendarme lying in wait for motorists at the same spot. However, this time, he was waived on. It was no problem, from the moral high ground as an innocent man, to make a point about harassment. However, when he was caught shortly afterwards in a speed trap by the same officer, it was a far bigger challenge to wriggle out of a fine.

"I was still driving a car that had been bought in the UK with right hand drive. The speedo was calibrated in miles per hour and not kilometres per hour. So, when I drove along a French road with a road sign showing a speed limit of 50, it was 50 Km per hour. I didn't think and kept to 50 on my speedo – which unfortunately was showing 50 miles per hour! Without realising it, I was speeding at just over 80 kilometres per hour."

This time, it was a fair cop. Francois was ushered by the triumphant officer onto a roadside caravan they were using to process errant motorists. He was left in the hands of a higher-ranking local policeman who, as luck would have it, was a regular customer at the restaurant. By coincidence, the officer had booked for a meal the following weekend. Having heard the mitigating circumstances regarding the speeding offence and the story about alleged harassment by the reporting officer, discretion was exercised. Accompanying the friendly warning was some guidance for Francois. He was advised not to look happy or smug as he left the caravan - to avoid any misunderstandings in the eyes of other offenders should their circumstances preclude such leniency. It was particularly difficult not to reveal any hint of satisfaction as he walked past the problematic officer!

It seemed that the campaign involved blanket checks on all motorist. Whilst feeling somewhat aggrieved at the constant stops, Francois understood that the motives underlying the inconveniences was for the greater good of road safety. It brought some perspective to the seemingly aggressive tactics. As word got round, business at the restaurant progressively increased. It seemed that he had the Midas touch. Good food was important. Value and affordability were also variables in determining success. Yet the personality of the restauranteur was also a factor in any detailed analysis of viability. Francois had the ability to ensure that the latter had a strong weighting when it came to results.

"Business soon became exceptionally good. We had eighty dining places inside and seventy outside. We were full every lunchtime. Not all our business clients were French. On Sundays, a lot of French families used to come. On the one hand, they were visiting a reputable and good quality restaurant, but on the other were reluctant to pay the price for good food. These days, that demand would be catered for by the large-scale pub food operations that have expanded in recent years in England and elsewhere."

As the restaurant's popularity grew, it began to attract more famous clients. This time, Francois initially had no idea that one of the diners in a corner of the room was a celebrity from the UK hit television series - Allo Allo. On the evening in question, some friends from his Willerby restaurant had called in to eat on their journey through

France to their holiday destination. Francois was unaware they had arrived. As he wandered through the dining area, talking casually to customers, one of the party from East Yorkshire called across to him, "Hey Francois, are you ignoring us?" Surprised by their presence - and devotees of the series will understand that I will say this only once - Francois went into 'Allo, Allo' mode mimicking Renee (Gordon Kaye) the café owner character in the UK Sitcom series. The stories are set in German-occupied France during the Second World War. In the programmes wife Edith, is unaware of Renee's affairs with his waitress. A regular singer in the Café, which is frequented by the Gestapo (Herr Flick), Edith's vocal skills leave much to be desired. Each character has a catchphrase. Enter Francois in a broken French accent so beautifully characterising Renee's voice.

"Oh Allo, I am just pissing through and I have seen some Germans shitting at people."

In the corner, the Brits were laughing hysterically at the very credible impression. What happened next was totally unexpected, unbelievable and although unscripted in the restaurant was a line that viewers throughout the UK would instantly recognise. "Renee, Oh Renee" cried a female voice from the other corner of the room. The French accent and line perfectly mimicked the voice of Edith in the TV series. All eyes in the restaurant turned to the lady in the corner whose face, if not dress, perfectly resembled the performer who was Edith in the TV series. Francois looked across at the table. Sitting there smiling at him was actress Carmen Silvera – Edith from the TV series! The Brits in the room were in awe at the coincidence. A star of the show was in the restaurant as Francois chose to mimic her TV husband.

"It was unbelievable that Carmen was in the restaurant at that time. I was not aware that it was her when I did an impression of Renee. In fact, we carried it on for a while because I asked her if I could take her into the "brushing cupboard" which was another of Renee's catchphrases. It was great fun and one of many coincidences in my career. We met again some years later when she came to Hull to perform the stage version of the TV series."

When the three years was over, Francois found himself extremely tired. The restaurant operation had been managed around himself and Sue, with staffing at a level that balanced good service with sound financial management. Although relationships with most French clients at Guines was exceptionally good, Francois understood that a growing number of French people were becoming less inclined to pay the price for dining-out.

"Some French people who go to restaurants think they own you as a waiter or restauranteur. Their attitude and approach can often be disrespectful and demeaning. I saw this a lot in those times when I visited other restaurants in France.

I saw waiters being treated like slaves by French diners. English customers are generally very relaxed with a great sense of humour. They are more likely to chat with the restaurant staff. In part, it may be because the French take their dining more seriously. It is said that they live to eat and that the English eat to live. Of course, that is a generalisation, because there are gourmets all over the world."

When it came to matters of 'tipping' when settling the bill, Francois came to some conclusions about his own experiences:

"From my experience, the Americans and the Germans were the best when it came to tips. I also saw this when Sue and I went on holiday in Europe. The Germans like to make sure they get the best service and because the waiters know they will be rewarded, they tend to focus on pleasing them before anyone else. In my opinion all customers should get the same good service."

❊ ❊ ❊

Whilst Sue and Francois were at Guines, they took a break and travelled to Lisle where they found a restaurant that had originated as an oyster stall and developed into a gastronomical institution which deservedly attracted a Michelin star. Noted for its good standards of service and seafood offerings, the establishment was a delight for lovers of fine food. As ever, restaurants of high repute attracted the rich and famous. As Sue and Francois sat enjoying their food, one of the waiters who was known to them from previous visits confided in a notable booking that was expected to arrive shortly. The expected guest was none other than a senior French politician who had guided new employment rules into law. She was a regular visitor to the restaurant. The booking was for twelve people at 8pm. A call had been received, asking if the time could be varied to 8.30pm. The irony was that the effect of the new legislation had caused the restaurant to clamp down on staff hours and opening times. As the evening wore on, it became clear that the party were going to be very late for their booking. At 9.30 a single person from group arrived explaining that the meeting they had attended was running late. Things soon turned sour as Francois observed:

"Sue and I realised as time went on that there was going to be a problem. The restaurant was under tighter financial pressure thanks to the legislation the lead guest had enacted. It got so late that staff were winding down the kitchen and making ready to close. The government minister finally arrived only to be told that service was no longer available. She was not happy and left red-faced. Politicians often make laws and manage to escape the consequences, thanks to their position. On this occasion, that was not the case."

As the end of three years at Guines approached, Francois and Sue took stock of the business. Trade was good. The benefits could be measured in Euros and working with a happy team, but the costs included a high degree of physical exhaustion with an associated risk to health. The project near Calais was always intended to be time-limited and an extended stay in France not even considered as a serious proposition. East Yorkshire was calling and a return to Hull was just what the doctor might order – especially given Francois' desire to ease off and run a smaller operation. Sue was in full agreement. In spite of the trade not being her favourite occupation, she had always supported her husband fully at every stage of his career. They both agreed that it was time for a change of scenery.

They say that a change is as good as a rest, but the restaurant trade is demanding anywhere in the world. The only way to put the 'rest' into restaurant is to build the business, employ a good team and successfully scale the operation so that others can be delegated responsibility with accountability at all levels. This is a pipe dream for most -with the danger that each change in the industry represents a trip from the fat into the frying pan. Yet, for Francois the life was in his blood. The interaction with customers was something that made him tick. The aim was to find a suitable work-life balance - and to ensure that the work element did not tax him too much as the years passed-by. As he waved goodbye to his team at Guines, Francois set his sights on a new venture in East Yorkshire - where he knew that a ready-made clientelle would welcome him with open arms.

Francois - the entertainer

KINGSTON ROAD

D espite the prospect of more hard work, the move to 159 Kingston Road in Willerby brought a really positive feel from being home again for both Sue and Francois. Although his country of birth was France, he had developed a close affinity with the English. Just a short walk from a newly acquired Willerby home, the former café at 159 Kingston Road was ideally situated in a leafy suburb to the west of Hull. They decided to set up their new restaurant venture at that location. Surrounded by middle-class dwellings and a nice run of shops with easy parking for customers in the surrounding area, it had the intrinsic advantage of being in the same catchment area of his previously successful enterprise in the Willerby Shopping Park - less than a mile away. The Francois brand was known in the area and had a regular following of devotees.

With the famous, hugely popular and extensive Hull Fair having packed up and gone, Christmas was but a few weeks away. There was no time to waste. Clearly, the festive season is the busiest and most lucrative period of the year for the restaurant industry. There was both a sense of urgency and a feeling of excitement as Sue and Francois arranged the tables and put up the decorations. The restaurant had 36 covers, was square in shape with a bar at the back – beyond which stood a well-appointed and spotlessly clean kitchen. In the dining area, white walls contrasted beautifully with the red tablecloths to give a warm feel to the place. With the sound of Edith Piaf in the background and the wooden flooring adding a layer of authenticity, it took only a small flight of imagination to transport any mildly inebriated diner into an authentic and classy eatery in the cobbled streets of any French town.

Arriving back in the area was a great thrill with the prospect of meeting old friends and developing the business again. Deciding on what to include in the menu was an interesting process. There was already a considerable understanding of local tastes from the previous enterprise in the Willerby Shopping Park. Francois and Sue set about the opportunity with enthusiasm, employing a team that they felt could meet the required standards, whether it be in the kitchen or serving customers. Francois was back in town - soon to be joined by Julienne - a chef he had employed in Guines.

Sue and Francois

Sue took on board a key role front of house. She adopted an iron fist in velvet glove approach with the staff – and on occasion also with customers. To the casual observer, it was a delight to experience. Although more engaged in the kitchen, Francois always found time to mix with the clients – and whenever possible to entertain them with the accordion. Once he'd augmented the staff by bringing Phil on board as an additional chef, Francois turned his attention to filling other vacancies. Although initially employed as a pot-washer, Callum Williams quickly caught the eye of his discerning boss. The youngster had potential and Francois instinctively knew it.

Having started his career in the kitchen at a local

bar, the young man already had practical experience of putting together pub food. His new job offered an invaluable insight into a higher level of cooking. His new boss had his roots in what had been France's top restaurant. The promising recruit was just starting his journey in the industry. Spurning the opportunity to continue schooling in the 6th Form, Callum commenced a formal NVQ Level 2 course at Hull College and had worked at the Wildfowler pub the evenings and weekends. He recalls:

"I began washing pots at the Wildfowler just before I'd turned sixteen. Within a month I had pretty much done most of the tasks in the kitchen. It was so busy, I found myself being asked to fill in for others when they were absent. Taking up a job washing pots might have seemed a step back on the face of it, but the chance to work for Francois was too good to miss. He had a terrific reputation and I felt I could learn so much in a dedicated restaurant setting. In my first job, pans were not exactly evident as it was a different operation. It was well run by very competent people, but Francois was my first experience of a professional restaurant kitchen."

The restaurant "Francois" was an instant success. Customers new and old came along to sample the combination of English and French fayre. Initially, the door opened in the mornings offering a café menu. However, this decision to extend the restaurants appeal had some unintended consequences that required remedial action. Francois recalled the situation, his voice betrayed traces of the frustration he felt at the time.

"The morning opening was a disaster for us. Ladies with prams would come in and park up for long periods – sometimes well into the afternoon. They would chat with friends for hours over a single cup of coffee. Some of the older people would sit reading a newspaper in the warm to save on heating at home. This was great for the customer, but for us it was not sustainable in business terms. Much as I liked them and was happy in their company, the practice interfered with lunchtime diners. I had no option but to stop the morning coffee shop."

Soon after the restaurant had opened, The Hull Daily Mail dispatched a respected food critic to review the fayre at Francois of Willerby. The reporter waxed lyrical about one of the desserts on offer - Pain Perdu or 'eggy bread' which earned the description - 'double scrumptious.' The basic dish and its variant toppings were described in great detail by the reporter - along with a promise to return the next day for more: 'In simple terms you take a couple of slices of bread, soak them in egg and milk and a drop of rum (the rum is optional for hard-up students!), fry or griddle them, and serve with toppings of your choice (jam and maple syrup were my favourites). Here it came with brown and white sugar to be smeared on, pancake style, plus a dollop of vanilla ice-cream.'

The dish had originated on the tables of French peasants back in the day and was concocted as a means of resuscitating stale bread. The item had been one of the most popular at La Ferme Gourmande. The write-up in the paper fizzed with superlatives about the service, describing Francois as a 'master' front of house taking the time to meet and greet and providing an object lesson in how things should be done. Describing the restaurant as one of the "hottest tickets in town," the critic described Francois' latest effort in the village as having "taken things to an even greater level." Perhaps the most popular dish when the restaurant was at the nearby Willerby Shopping Park was rabbit casserole. This didn't work so well at the new location. Vegetarian options were available, but as Sue recalls, one vegetarian customer had a curious request each time he came.

"We had a very charming gentleman in his sixties who regularly came with his wife. He declared that he was a vegetarian and always asked to see the vegetarian menu. Yet, his order was always the boeuf bourguignon – obviously a meat dish. When I queried it with him, he'd always smile and with a wink say it was the (non-existent) *vegetarian* boeuf bourguignon he wanted! He simply couldn't resist it! Another customer always made a big point of telling Sue that he was on a diet. Yet his order always contained either extra fries or mash. When it came to the dessert, he'd tell her not to make the mistake of turning up with a small portion of pudding – usually the "Crepe Francois. Occasionally, he'd order seconds. We were flattered as well as amused. The same customer constantly made a point of criticising the 'Tarte Au Pomme' – or apple pie French style. A lover of the English version of the dessert, he accused the French of 'murdering' the dish which we make with a lot of apple content and strips of pastry across the top. It was all expressed in good humour, but there was no joking about the sincerity of the protest. I already knew that the English take their apple pies very seriously!"

Although he spent a lot of time supervising in the kitchen, Francois was, as ever, the ultimate showman greeting clients, and chatting to them. Periodically, but especially throughout the Christmas festive periods, special evenings were organised with guest bands and performers. Elvis or Buddy Holly tribute acts were particularly popular. Towards the end of the evening, Francois would appear with a quiz followed by a few songs on his trusty accordion. These evenings were always fully subscribed , highly valued by the diners and recognised as bringing something very special to the night life in the area.

In his kitchen duties, Francois concentrated on grilling the steaks, checking the food and plating dishes. He also made sauces. Julienne cooked meats and created other sauces, whilst Phil concentrated on starters and desserts. The restaurant relied on fresh local produce - with no compromise on quality. It was the Troisgros principles again in operation. To remain competitive, he relied on his personality to charm suppliers - in order to remain competitive on price. In the background, Callum continued his catering studies whilst working with Francois. It was a perfect combination for a budding chef. As Callum recalls:

"I learned a lot from Francois. Already, from my father's advice, I knew that a career in catering meant hard graft. I had no problem with that. I saw Francois' enthusiasm, his jovial character and great passion for customer service. Discipline was an important part of the work as he had very high standards. Despite this ethic, he was kind to me and adopted a fatherly approach – even when I erred. Whenever possible he allowed me to get involved in cooking – but it was limited because he already had two chefs. Francois knew that I was a dedicated Hull City fan and whenever possible he would allow me to attend home matches, stretching the start time beyond 5pm so I could see all of the game.

On one occasion, when the team were in the Premier League, I wanted to have time off to attend an away game at Manchester United. I crossed the line really because I didn't arrive at the restaurant until 8.30pm. He wasn't happy as I'm sure he felt let down. There was no conversation and I found myself just washing pots. At the end of the shift, he asked me to follow him as he wanted a word. Knowing his record on discipline, I feared getting the sack. But when he started to speak, it was in a fatherly tone. He understood how important the game was to me but firmly made the point about the duty to work and colleagues. I rated him highly as an employer and as a person."

When reminded of the incident, Francois paid tribute to his former employee:

"Callum was a young talent. He was keen, hardworking and was always looking to learn something. I admired his work ethic and I saw something in him. I felt that he could go a long way in the profession."

In survey after survey, when questioned about the quality of their management, employees rate highly the manager's interest and care in their personal circumstances and development. With Francois, whilst insisting on the highest standards from staff, he always took an interest in their welfare and fair remuneration. These traits we in part natural, but also reflected the culture of his French employers in teen years.

Contributors to the Trip Advisor website gave generally excellent reviews but some picked up some classic incidents, which years later still raise a smile. Sue was always supportive of her husband and they made a dedicated pair. However, it was no secret that the restaurant business was not her first love.

By the time, 159 Kingston Road came along, her tolerance of the catering scene was wearing quite thin. Yet she persevered, knowing how important her support was to Francois. Her contribution to the business was always important and her efforts immensely valued.

Table setting at Francois Restaurant in Kingston Road Willerby

To allow the maximum number of guests to enjoy the cuisine, Francois tried to use every inch of floor space to accommodate the tables. Sometimes, this left the aisle width at a premium. And it came to pass that on one occasion, a cramped diner left her bag in the walkway. On passing by several times in the restricted pathway to take orders, Sue tired of the obstacle. Her remedial action was to the point and effective. However, the lapse in customer service skills was exposed when the client took to on-line media to complain that Sue had simply booted her bag out of the way! It was almost a Fawlty Towers moment. The Troisgros brothers would not have approved. However, the cameo may have raised a smile. Even Francois had his moments. Entering the restaurant one lunchtime, one diner saw the funny side of Francois uncharacteristically in a rage.

"I walked into the empty restaurant and witnessed a red-faced Francois slamming the telephone down with vigour. He said that he hated the (bleeping) French. I'd never seen him so mad, Apparently, he'd been on the phone quite a long time on an international call with some petty tax official in Calais who'd obviously wound him up. He soon calmed down though."

Family friend Jacques Mielhan fully understood the problem, having himself experienced the delights of French bureaucracy at its worst. He was also severe in his criticism of the service across the channel:

"Dealing with the French pension people is really frustrating. They regularly request documents as proof of entitlement. You would think that a doctor might be qualified, but I am required to go to a solicitor every six months and they certify that I am still alive. The French authorities seem to have a paranoia about claims being made by a corpse. In the UK a single phone call is usually enough to resolve any questions. It got so bad that, for the small

161

pension I was receiving from my home country, it was hardly worth claiming if solicitor's fees are taken into account. To Francois, any mention of the French pension people is like a red rag to a bull. We do understand that they have to be careful to avoid pension fraud - but there are limits."

Another guest witnessed a Fawlty Towers moment involving a harassed Sue, who was dealing with a customer at the till which was located at the rear of the restaurant. She'd spied two people in coats near to the entrance door. At that moment, a waitress appeared from the rear kitchen carrying two dishes for expectant guests. Not wishing to lose the custom of clients at the entrance, she ordered the waitress to put the dishes down and go immediately to welcome the customers. In fact, they were leaving the restaurant after their meal. Protestations from the waitress were curtly brushed aside and the rapped instructions dutifully carried out. This left several people somewhat bemused. The expectant diners, salivating for the dishes which had been so near, saw their food dumped on the counter. The guest paying his bill wondered why members of his party who had just donned their coats prior to leaving were now again being welcomed in by the waitress. These days, people will pay good money for such themed entertainment. The story did not have a Manuel element - and for that everyone was grateful. Nobody mentioned the war! Callum was a keen observer of Sue's mild idiosyncrasies.

"At first I thought she just hated being there. Certainly, she did not suffer fools gladly. I didn't get a good impression at the start. She could be charming, but often the grumpiness came through. Yet, I also saw a completely different side to her on occasions when away from the business. She could be extremely charming, thoughtful, kind and caring. Both she and Francois got on very well though and that was also nice to see."

After a couple of years working at the Francois restaurant, Callum found himself coming to the end of his catering studies. To complete the course, he needed to complete a new work placement. Francois recommended that he select the Michelin Star restaurant at Wintringham Fields. Located in nearby North Lincolnshire, the establishment had earned a national reputation for the quality of its cuisine. The 16th century former farmhouse is not only set in a county known for its agriculture, but also has its own small-holding where animals are reared and vegetables grown for consumption in the restaurant. Whilst there, Callum was offered a full-time job. It was a no-brainer to accept. In a sense, he was following in his boss's footsteps by opening up an opportunity to further learn from the best in the business. So, it was au-revoir for the time being, but he and Francois would work together again in the future. As time went by, the Francois restaurant grew more and more popular. Business clients, locals and diners from farther afield flocked to sample the food. As word got around, corporate customers began looking to book large groups. It wasn't possible to cope with catering on this scale in the space available.

"At Willerby Shopping Park, we had lots of covers. We were limited at 159 Willerby Road because space was at a premium. It was enough for us because we wanted to wind down a little. It was still very hard work, of course. Within the overall English and French cuisine on offer I tried to make sure that we catered for vegetarians and vegans as a lot of restaurants neglected such diners. We also had to bear in mind that some people do not like what they would describe as exotic dishes like frogs' legs – popular though they were with some customers. Allergies were becoming an important consideration and on occasions it felt like I was working in hospital catering! We also began to realise a growing trend that people wanted to eat earlier in the evening. Unless we laid on a special entertainment, things were winding down after 9pm."

Clients at 159 Kingston Road knew that being treated to a rare taste of France. Excellent food was being served at fair prices. The atmosphere was friendly, romantic and laced the with the humour and personality of an authentic host. With occasional cabaret nights, the restaurant's offer was a real asset to the area. Eventually, after six years at 159 Kingston Road, Francois began feeling increasingly tired with the pressure of work. Overheads were increasing and impinging on profits, He began to think of retirement – or at least a real break. Although he did not own the premises, intending purchasers were yet again willing to offer an inducement to pave the way for their taking over the space. As if by tradition, as one door closed, another opened in the shape of customer Roland Craft who for some time had wanted to enlist Francois talents in his own enterprise. Mr Craft, who sadly passed-away in August 2016 had taken ownership of the Monks Walk pub in nearby Beverley. His great vision of a pub, restaurant, beer garden and small hotel appealed to Francois. The onerous responsibilities of running his own business in an increasingly difficult financial climate would seemingly be replaced by stable and less stressful employment. He had extensive experience in all the required areas and the scale of the enterprise did not suggest that it would be necessary to pedal under severe pressure. However, the role of general manager was to be fraught with problems that were not in his gift to control. From his point of view, it would turn out to be a poisoned chalice.

MONKS WALK & MILLHOUSE

T he Monks Walk pub is located in historic Highgate in Beverley. The road (previously known as Old Highgate or London Road) stretches from Wednesday Market down to Minster Yard North – where parts of the historic Beverley Minster have stood since 700 AD. The pub building is reputed to date back to 1270 with developments taking place throughout the Medieval period. Although it was previously known as the Green Dragon, the passageway in the centre of the building was said to have been utilised by Monks as a short-cut. This gave the inspiration for the pub's new name.

To realise his vision for the premises, the owner Roland Craft enlisted the support of Francois who agreed to take up the post of general manager. His role was to initiate, oversee and run the front-end restaurant, bar and cocktail lounge operation. Meanwhile, Mr Craft took the lead in the building conversion and overall financial management of the enterprise. There was a developing plan to convert upstairs space into hotel accommodation. It was felt that the building's historical background and proximity to the Minster would prove to be a great attraction for visitors. During the works, particularly in the upper areas, tradesmen discovered startling evidence of the building's historic origins. Historic England visited the site and declared that the original walls should remain on view and be covered only by protective Perspex material. Having already secured Francois' services, there followed a frustrating period of building delays in no small degree caused by historic preservation imperatives Keen to meet the projected opening date and ensure that all the necessary organisational matters under his responsibilty flowed logically and in a timely manner, Francois found himself more and more frustrated. The stress grew steadily and culminated in a serious health setback. Yet, he initially dealt with his medical crisis in a worryingly relaxed manner. It could easily have cost him his life.

"I'm sorry to say that the seemingly never-ending project was by far, the worst experience of my life. The delays were infuriating. Nothing seemed to be happening at the pace needed to meet the opening date. Serving and restaurant staff had to be recruited and trained. Equipment had to be made ready for use and all sorts of systems put in place. This became problematic as continuing delays blighted the building works. Finally, enough progress had been made so that the bar and restaurant could open."

Unfortunately, things were still far from satisfactory in terms of meeting the standards that Francois had set the organisation. In the end, the stress upon him reached fever-pitch and he suffered a stroke two months after launch. It happened one Sunday morning at the pub when he was in the company of the Assistant Manager:

"I felt as if my eyes were going to pop out. There was no response from my left arm and my speech was slurred. Also, I felt pain in my leg."

Despite the sudden onset and severity of the symptoms, Francois refused to allow an ambulance to be called. Instead, he decided to wait and see if he might feel better. Retiring to his office, he slept for the next two hours, still unable to speak coherently. He had experienced the classic symptoms of a stroke. The correct action was to have responded to the symptoms by urgently calling 999 for paramedic assessment, emergency treatment and admission to hospital. The FAST pneumonic is for Face Arms Speech and Time – the latter being a critical factor in survival rates and prognosis. In failing to allow immediate emergency care, Francois had placed his life at serious and immediate risk. Foolishly sticking it out, he risked sudden deterioration and an even more serious attack. Had that happened, the likelihood of fatal consequences would have been extremely high. Although his speech returned within six hours, he remained at grave risk. That evening, he spoke with GP who strongly advised immediate admission to hospital. Yet, it was the next day before Francois finally presented himself for examination at the Accident & Emergency Department at the Hull Royal Infirmary.

Doctors were aghast at the delay between symptoms first arising and examination by a health professional. They ordered an immediate MRI scan to aid diagnosis and measure the extent of any possible damage. Faced with entering the full body scanner, Francois refused. His long-standing fear of confined spaces was almost certainly due to his teenage experience as a passenger in a fatal car crash. In that event, he had been helpless to affect the accident and had ended up trapped in a confined space. Later in life, he found himself unable to enter a lift or be in any restricted space – especially if unaccompanied. Despite its possible life-saving role in diagnosis and treatment, entering the scanner tube was impossible to face. He went home on a presumed diagnosis, suitable medication and appropriate advice. There was little else that the doctors could do in the circumstances. This was not the first time that Francois had experienced the phobia. The first occasion had been in a lift that had jammed between floors. He'd been surprised at his own panic reaction. Then some time afterwards, he'd found himself locked in a restaurant toilet. This time he experienced a severe phobic response with a waiter ending up kicking-in the door.

Although helped by a hypnotherapist in Hull, the problem remained. It got to a point that flying became impossible and car journeys were increasingly affected. To try and eradicate his phobia, Francois consulted the famous London-based therapist Paul McKenna. His claim to fame included helping Stephen Fry to lose weight and assisting David Walliams in a Channel swim. He also gave treatment to Russell Brand for addictions. McKenna used a new therapy called 'Havening' to beat stress, cure addictions, deal with post-traumatic stress, help with bereavements issues and neutralise phobias. The system involved using a series of eye movements as well as tapping or stroking arms. The aim is to encourage the release of brain chemicals to break down negative emotions and anxiety. Anyone can use the therapy, it is claimed. Francois enrolled on a seminar and travelled to London, hoping that he could gain some benefit from the experience. Forty of fifty people attended the event. Paul McKenna led the two-day course and he was assisted by others in his team. It was by chance that Francois was selected by the principal for one-to-one sessions:

"Paul asked me about my phobias and I explained them to him. Then he took them one by one and we worked on them together. People were hypnotised in such a way that they still knew what they were doing. We were told that we would not be forced to do anything we didn't want to do and would still be in control. On my one-to-one, Paul pointed to a box, told me there was a rat inside and asked if I would like to stroke it. I refused. He asked how much anxiety I felt on a scale of ten - with ten being the worst. I replied ten. He then moved his eyes and waved his hand in an up and down stroke and then asked me how I felt. I replied six! I touched the rat. The process was repeated with a python and with the same results. When it moved on to the lift, I was extremely worried. At first, he came in the lift with me and kept trying to improve the anxiety score by his method. However, I still couldn't go in the lift alone. I did get some benefit from the weekend, but he concluded that the horrific car crash I'd had as a teenager had seriously affected me. When it came to going-in the MRI scanner at the hospital, I just couldn't manage to do it. I've spoken to people since then and they've told me their experiences in an MRI and it doesn't sound so bad – but for me it was a massive problem at the time."

Fortunately for the Monks Walk, Francois had already made a crucial appointment. Former employee Callum Williams had been recruited back from Wintringham Fields where he had gained invaluable insights and experience on fine-dining techniques. It was an inspired appointment. Despite the relative inexperience of the 22 year-old, backed by the Monks Walk owner, Francois entrusted the young man with the role of Head Chef. Having studied the art under the brilliant Colin McGurran, his development had progressed along all the right lines. He was now ready to take the next step in his career. His previous positive experience of working with Francois meant that the arrangement had every chance of success.

Callum Williams at The Monks Walk in 2013

Looking back, Francois recalls that he had no hesitation at the time:

"I saw that Callum had lots of potential when he worked for me at 157 Kingston Road. Wintringham Fields gave him important insights into how a top-flight restaurant operates. After speaking to him, I was sure that he was ready for what would be required at Monks Walk. Although, he was given a leading role, the plan was for me to oversee the menus and retain overall control. I saw that he was a perfectionist. This was exactly what was needed. We were on the same page with standards. Callum was a pleasant character, totally grounded with a good business head and clearly had talent in the kitchen. He was very inventive and was the most outstanding young talent I have ever worked alongside."

In the event, Francois' stroke left a huge void at the top of the operation and the pub and restaurant had to operate without him. However, his prodige was perfectly capable of taking up the challenge. At Winteringham Fields, Callum had enthusiastically worked long hours, and he had absorbed every moment of that time to learn. He vividly recalls the time when he found himself taking full responsibility for all the kitchen operations.

"It was really unfortunate that Francis suffered such an event. As he got over the stroke, he kept in touch and was always supportive. I had full responsibility for the menus and the operation of the kitchen. It was challenging, but then again, it was my dream to be running a kitchen. Happily, Francois slowly recovered and eventually returned to work. He did then bring-in some changes to the menu. Whilst I felt these were ambitious in terms of the number of dishes against the budget allowed, I respected his views."

On assuming his intended role as General Manager, Francois was far from happy about the circumstances under which he was working.

"It seemed to me that the finances of the Monks Walk were becoming ever tighter. The project to develop the beer-garden and rooms was still under way and I suspect that this may have led to financial pressures on the owner."

Whatever the underlying cause, sadly the relationship between Francois and Roland Craft became increasingly strained. Although an employee, the Francois brand was integral to the restaurant's marketing thrust. His name on the windows was enough to draw publicity and past customers. For a while, Francois made every effort to try and make the arrangement work. Clients, drawn to the Francois brand and the cuisine on offer were certainly in a seventh heaven. Head chef Callum was certainly delivering the goods. Clients were delighted with the quality and value. One distinguished GP guest, who had dined with his wife after being recommended by a colleague was so pleased that on the way home he parked his car and rang the friend who had told him about the food. He waxed lyrical over the whole experience. The location did have a slight drawback insofar as parking availability in that area of Beverley was not the best. Whilst a few spaces were available at the rear of the premises, most guests would have to walk some distance to reach the venue. Taxi or a brisk walk were the obvious solution for some locals – but most guests came from other towns and villages where such journeys might be expensive. One of the plans that the owner had in mind, was the development of a cocktail lounge. This was to cater especially for younger local clients. With a bar offering fine ales, the project had a wide potential.

* * *

The historic Monks Walk was not without haunting tales. It had a fascinating history and a 'past' - but many wondered if it also has a 'presence.' Ghost walks are popular in Beverley and the pub was firmly on the stop-off list for devotees. Francois recalls strange goings-on during his relatively short period at the place. His office was located at the rear of the building to the left of the passageway that historically had been used by Monks from the Minster.

"One night I was sitting in my office about 8pm and I heard a strange noise. It was coming from upstairs. Something was causing the bare floorboards to creak. It was if someone was walking in the room. At the same time, I heard another sound. It sounded as if a box was being dragged across the room. I went upstairs to investigate but the door was locked. It is normally left open. It felt strange. Very strange. Some of the staff lived in an opposite building, so I went to fetch one of them and explained what had had happened. He brought his dog, in case there was an intruder. As we stood outside the door, the dog began crying. Animals apparently have an ability to sense or smell things that we can't. When I tried the door, it opened! In itself, that seemed spooky. The dog had clearly sensed something. There was nobody inside the room. However, we did find some bottles of wine and glasses lying around. No sooner had we gone back down the staircase, we heard a bang from the same room. When we went back upstairs again to check what had happened, we found that the glasses had been moved. We didn't see anybody in the room - and there was no rational explanation for what had happened."

Locals at the pub often recounted it's ghostly history. It seems that one of the past landlords would leave a full glass of beer on the bar last thing in the evening - only to find it was empty in the morning. Francois tried the 'beer test' several times and on one occasion found the glass empty in the morning. Although to the best of his knowledge, he had been last one out and first one in, the owner also had a key for the place. He denied accessing the premises and was poker-faced about it at the time. Francois remained unsettled at the Monks Walk. His serious illness had further added to the feeling of gloom. The venture was turning out to be a long way from what it said on the tin! The most frustrating aspect was that he had no control over the continuous hold-ups that dogged the development of the wider project that included a beer-garden and rooms to let on the first floor.

"After my stroke, I was at a pretty low ebb. For quite a while, I was unable to work. Rehabilitation seemed to be very slow. It affected me both physically and mentally. I was like a fish out of water.

It was a depressing situation and I wondered if I would ever work again."

As had happened several times before at key moments in his career, Francois received an offer from an influential and powerful local business-man. This time, it was Mark Ciuffetelli, owner of both the Millhouse restaurant at Skidby and The Country Park Hotel at Hessle. Francois recalls the approach from Mr Ciufattelli:

"Mark is the son of my late friend and former boss Franco Ciuffatelli. He learned about my ill-ness and understood that I loved my work and very kindly stepped in with a job offer that was sensitive to my advancing years and health issues. I wanted only part-time work and hoped to avoid undue stress. His kind, thoughtful and sensitive approach was to be respected and I readily agreed to work with him."

The parting of the ways with the Monks Walk was understandable. Stress and high-level pres-sures were the last thing that Francois needed, given the health problems. In any case, it was al-ways planned that Callum would eventually take up the reigns. It was also the case that Francois still had a lot to offer - and Mark had appeared with a generous plan that captured the needs of the mo-ment.

The arrangement saw Francois taking a lead role in greeting customers at the Millhouse. His task was to ensured that their entire experience was positive. Later, he also worked in a similar role at the Country Park pub restaurant and hotel situated on Hessle foreshore in the shadow of the Humber Bridge towers.

Francois pictured at The Country Park bar, restaurant and hotel

Mark Ciuffatelli, himself a trained chef, was rich in praise for the contribution Francois had made to his businesses.

"Francois is a real character and had worked with my late father earlier in his career. They had a mutual respect for each other. He is old school, polite, always smartly dressed and meticulous in terms of standards of behaviour. He has a very strong service ethic. Yet, he has a great sense of humour and a fantastic ability to engage and resonate with customers of all ages and widely varying backgrounds. At the Millhouse in Skidby, we offer food at a high standard, cooked as close to perfection as we can get it. This approach demands great chefs, excellent levels of service and a very personal approach. When I heard he had been ill, I knew he'd be wanting to recover and find a role somewhere without too much stress. Francois is a natural with customers. His reassuring, calm and highly professional presence front of house was a perfect fit with the top-class image we wanted to project. I felt that bringing him on board was great for him - and for us. Leading into 2018, our Country Park operation had received major investment. We developed the pub and built in an exceptional food offer. The facilities were also perfect for wedding receptions and other functions. Francois was part of our launch and development and worked between The Millhouse and The Country Park. Staff and customers alike at both places love Francois. He is funny, with just the right amount of banter. Yet, along with the humour he has a steely attentiveness to the needs of clients. He is gifted in all these respects."

When at the prestigious Millhouse, Francois became more and more aware of the now intense attention needed for diners with allergies – some which could seriously affect health – and in the extreme be life-threatening. Emergency planning, staff training and communication between the restaurant and its clients were vital elements in ensuring the safety of customers at risk. Customer service was always a paramount consideration for

Francois. The standards had been inculcated at Les Freres Troisgros where Michelin stars dictated the highest levels of excellence throughout the operation. Yet clients can sometimes be unreasonable and unrealistic. Like the woman in the Fawlty Towers TV sitcom who demanded a better view from her room, there are limits to what fairly can be expected – even if the finest establishments.

"I recall a lady client once being unhappy with the choice available in what was an extensive menu – including vegetarian and vegan options. However, nothing was to her complete liking. She listed twenty-one different things that she could not eat. I tried to find something suitable, but it was all to no avail. She then accused me of not trying hard enough! It was at this point that, for once, I lost my patience and suggested that she perhaps try having a browse in the field outside - in case there was something out there that took her fancy! "

Francois 2018 at The Country Park, Hessle

It is the case that food allergies have risen in recent years. Scientists are not agreed as to the causes of this, but clearly allergic reactions are of serious concern - especially since some can cause health emergencies and even fatalities. Restaurants are not obliged to serve clients who present with food allergies. However, if they do agree to provide service, a number of legal responsibilities come into play. Diners with allergies should aquaint themselves with the restaurant's published food information and wherever possible follow reliable health guidlines and advice - whenever possible speaking to the food establishment beforehand. The arrangement with Mark was not especially long-lasting, despite the seeming perfect fit between the genial Frenchman, the high-class Millhouse brand and a thoughtful employer. It seemed that in his advancing years, Francois was having a mid-life crisis! He still longed to be running his own show, but at least more in control of events to which he had lent his name and had taken responsibility. It was an inevitable and perhaps insoluble tension. The years were catching up on a character that relied on energy and endurance to meet the high standards that he had set himself. But was there another curtain-call for the showman?

✻ ✻ ✻

"After I left the Millhouse, I did work alongside a Willerby Square café/restaurant owner for a short time. We agreed that I would lend my name to the restaurant on certain evenings. Although I would work front of house, it was agreed that I could determine the menu, provide staff supervision and also monitor kitchen standards. The arrangement did result in the appearance of many of my former clients."

Francois was over the moon to be meeting up with many of his former customers. They were what made him tick. The banter with was forever a joy. Providing them with great food and service was his mission.

"It was great to be back working in Willerby where I had spent so many years of my career, but it could never be the same as it was when it was my own business. Running a restaurant requires almost all your time and energy. I had this growing feeling that it was time to wind-down."

In early 2020 the global covid-19 pandemic caused severe disruption to the hospitality sector and effectively drove the eternal come-back kid into a domestic kitchen environment. It was the golden opportunity to recover and reflect.

THE LONG & WINDING-DOWN ROAD

Throughout his life, Francois made every effort to keep in touch with many colleagues in the trade and whenever possible, made regularly visits restaurants to chat with old friends and enjoy the food on offer. He is often seen with a coffee and a morning newspaper in local Willerby cafes. In relishing the opportunity to chat, he allows himself free rein to muse over many topical subjects with anyone that will listen.

"The continental lifestyles very much embrace the café culture. You can see it all over France and in other Mediterranean towns and cities. British tourists abroad saw this and whenever the weather permits, like to recreate it over here. With climate change, it will develop more and more. The covid-19 pandemic threw a bit of a spanner in the works. Many restaurants and cafés have closed permanently. Others have struggled, relying on offering takeaways to survive. People worked from home and if this develops into a long-term preferred way of working, then city businesses reliant on office clients will have to adapt."

Enjoyment in being in and around cafés and restaurants is clearly a throwback to the sunny childhood days in his grandma's café Midi when life was full of pleasure. He loved listening to the locals chatting in a relaxed way. Life was stress-free and full of mysteries to be explored. Given the fast-paced modern lifestyle and the toll of long hard years in the restaurant trade, the opportunity to slow down was not just desirable, but for Francois - a health imperative.

Yet set against this, despite being over the statutory retirement age, Francois still hankered for at least some involvement in the restaurant trade. Drawing the balance between avoiding stress and his natural wish to engage with clients was an extremely difficult tension to resolve. Over the years, he made many trips back to his native land and still shows much affection for the country – despite his extremely negative pronouncements on the bureaucratic inertia that appears endemic across France. There are some justifications for his comments. France is perhaps the prime example of a bureaucratic democracy. Public spending accounts for well over half of the country's gross domestic product (GDP). In order to enforce over 400,000 standards end statutes, a multiplicity of agencies, some with overlapping missions, conspire to soak up 84 billion euros in overhead costs.

"Some people say that you have to laugh at the French system. Sometimes I have almost cried – but not with laughter. On occasions, I have had to deal with French bureaucrats - and it is no joke. Frustration is a terrible thing and being kept waiting on an International call is not funny. You get thrown from pillar to post and everyone passes the buck. To be fair, it is getting a bit like this over here because as banks close, you are dealing with a remote call centre. And you can face ages just pressing buttons, listening to options and never ever speaking to anyone. It is a sort of electronic bureaucracy but the bureaucrats are now artificial intelligence bots!" You can't sell them a coffee or offer them a discount to visit your restaurant!"

At the heart of his culinary journey was French cuisine. It was his Royal Flush in the game. It was the ubiquitous and reliable skeleton key to open the doors of opportunity. Yet his offerings were never exclusively purist. His menus were always aimed to provide a broad appeal. This turned out to be the formula for success and it was based on the Francois signature style of remaining close to the customer base. He knew what they liked. Clients could always rely on the offering of frog's legs and beef bourguignon. The showman knew how to create sauces and flambe a steak at your table. Yet more exotic creations were deliberately absent. Avante Garde was never on the menu.

French cuisine has developed over many centuries with the cultures of neighbouring countries influencing the development of its own traditions as interpreted in the various regions. Yet, in the

17th century there was a shift to an indigenous French style. Cheese and wine always played an important part in the French taste. 20th Century Haute Cuisine was not easy to follow by cooks in a home environment and left out much of the local culinary character. However, the French style was ever evolving with the appearance of nouvelle cuisine (new cuisine). Yet the term was not new and the introduction of foreign influences hardly innovative. In essence, the late twentieth century drift was towards simplification and the reduction in cooking times for seafood and vegetables to preserve natural flavours. The use of fresh ingredients also became a totem of the new wave. Shorter menus were brought in. Strong meat & game marinades and heavy sauces were excluded in favour of using fresh herbs, good quality butter and lemon juice.

Haute Cuisine was rejected in favour of regional influences, which were openly embraced once more. Kitchens began using modern equipment – including microwave ovens. Importantly, chefs turned to the dietary requirements of their customers as a starting point when it came to the development of menus.

❊ ❊ ❊

In his short time at the Troisgros restaurant, where current and future icons of the culinary world were operating, Francois was embedded with the notion that the customer is king. They bestowed upon him the basic culinary and service standards and values that were the bedrock of his own journey in the trade. The dynasty Troisgros continues in France through descendants and in various locations. It is an ever-developing brand reflecting on past influences and at the same time never being afraid to test new directions. Although, Francois spent a relatively short period under the tutelage of the iconic family and its students, the principles and the disciplines were firmly embedded and formed the foundations of everything that followed.

"Of course, I understand the variety that can be offered as French cuisine. It has evolved over time and you can pick and choose what you put on the menu as French. It is very difficult to make money in any business and to do so you have to keep prices affordable but ensure that the customer really enjoys the food that you offer. If you were to ask, what cuisine did I offer? I would answer that, understanding the various tastes that clients have demonstrated, I have always offered some dishes that most people would recognise as French, cooked the French way. I have always embraced the value of local fresh produce whether it be vegetables, meat or game. There is no compromise on that. Generally, those "French" dishes I have had on my menus were adapted a little to reflect the English taste. It is no different to the cuisines of other countries where their people have set up shop over here. Chinese dishes are extremely popular, but they always have many dishes with a slant to the British taste. If you go to China and sample the food offered to local people over there, you will see that it is a world away from the 'Chinese' dishes offered over here. Whilst the difference in what I offer and what you might get in France are not great, to be successful you need to listen to how the clients react. The classic example of this was the failed attempt to offer nouvelle cuisine at the Willerby Manor all those years ago. Importantly, the management adapted quickly to the client feedback. It was what I had advocated and what I have always borne in mind. The food offered on the menu must of course reflect on what the customer is looking for or what they might find acceptable as a new culinary experience."

Looking back, the interpersonal skills and personality that shone so brightly in Roanne have been the sure ingredient that has helped clear seemingly impossibly high hurdles throughout a long and successful career. Happy clients became friends. And when it mattered, those friends shook hands and became the catalyst for a new direction. The showman was irrepressible. Whilst contemporaries concentrated on developing their reputations in the kitchen first and foremost, Francois seconded that focus to satisfying his desire to spend more time at the front of house. Knowing how to cook and present exceptional food was vital. Connecting with the client and listening to feedback, he felt, was also critical. His brand and the success that developed was all about balancing the two imperatives. Although the time he spent at Les Freres Troisgros was relatively short, his apprenticeship taught him the basic skills. He learned to respect people, to pay attention to detail and maintain the highest possible standards in all departments. The importance of supreme hygiene became the touchstone of his operations. He learned the value of being organised, the necessity for teamwork and the principles of customer service. All of this was embedded in his work and style. With some exceptions, Francois now mourns the deterioration of standards in what he now routinely sees in the general restaurant trade – both in terms of the food, hygiene and service.

"It is a sign of the times, I am afraid. Young people looking for jobs in waiting routinely do not respond to advice even about the basics. In some restaurants, they greet customers, including older clients, as "mate," "buddy," or "pal." Perhaps less disrespectful is the widespread use of the word "guys," It may be acceptable or bearable for clients of fast-food establishments and takeaways, but in a professional restaurant, I still want to experience higher standards. In recent times, many young people attend an interview scruffily dressed, totally unprepared and with a very casual couldn't care less approach. They don't want to work long hours or weekends. I routinely see clients being served glasses or cups after the waiting employee has placed their fingers on the upper part of the vessel. Often it is not noticed by the customer, but for me this is a sure way to pass bacteria from hand to mouth. These imperatives were highlighted during the covid pandemic – but were always important because other bacteria and viruses are always around us. Anyone with standards would almost certainly have doubts about returning to any restaurant that had lax hygiene standards. Shoddy hygiene practices are the result of poor training - or an employee that has no interest in doing a good job."

Francois maintains that high standards of hygiene in the kitchen and throughout a restaurant establishment is not only the absolute basic requirement for food safety, but it is the litmus test for whether to even consider eating in the place at all. Although he has always enjoyed exceptionally good customer relations, he has several pet hates when it comes to talking about a minority of clients at his restaurants. Top of the list is the clients who eat all the food and then lodge a complaint that something was not up to scratch.

"If there is a problem with the food, we always urge clients to let us know. More than that they will, as a matter of routine, be asked by staff whether everything is ok. I find it hard to understand when someone the complains about the food after having previously said that it was ok. For sure, some customers will complain simply in the hope that they will get something knocked off the bill. This is fraudulent and it is getting more and more common. Really, it is futile because most restaurants will ask if the food is ok once the customer has begun the meal. If they answer " yes," then unless there are exceptional circumstances, no discount is appropriate - because they have accepted the food delivered to the table."

In recent years, audiences at home have been drawn to watch all the food programmes that appear on the TV schedules. High end supermarkets are full of exotic ingredients and an array of magazines are published with recipes galore from countries around the world. Yet at the same time fast food establishments multiply like flies. Francois sees this as a dangerous invasion of madness upon common sense. In the UK and increasingly in other countries, obesity has become a major threat to the nation's health. Society has changed over the years so that people do not shop for healthy food or cook in a healthy way. It is a problem of convenience rather than economics. Eating a healthy diet can be much cheaper. It just needs a little time. The trouble is that some people would rather get a takeaway because it saves doing any cooking. Washing up is eliminated by tossing the cartons into a bin. In some cases, its laziness. Others find it difficult to manage the time needed to fulfil their employment commitments, look after children and do the housework."

These issues and arguments are well rehearsed and rising on the political agenda as government responds to public concern and the dramatically rising cost of healthcare. The authorities are looking to find ways of controlling sugar levels in drinks. Food labelling is improving - so that any interested shoppers can make more informed choices. However, the underlying social issues and fast food culture remain an impediment to progress. Francois believes that much more needs to be done:

"If you walk through any supermarket and carefully examine the labels, you will start to understand that the threats to health are both real and in fact almost unavoidable. If a shopper eliminates products that contain preservatives, high sugar levels and unhealthy fat content the range of products on offer could probably fill only a corner grocery shop that you would find in the old days. Discerning shoppers in the supermarket, looking for healthy options might find themselves drawn towards the fruit and vegetable sections. There they will find beautiful fruits, the appearance of which would not disgrace a stock photo website. Of uniform size and colour, they have mostly been cultivated to such a level using chemical sprays."

This reality check of the modern world represents a quantum fall in standards when compared to the days back in Bourg de Thizy when

everything was grown in a family garden or purchased fresh from local organic farmers. Of course,
governments and those interested in population
health are waking up to the dangers of too much
sugar, salt, fat and other unhealthy ingredients in
the modern diet. This is not to state that people
always lived healthy lifestyles back in the day. Exercise, sleep patterns, living conditions, genetics
and alcohol consumption and other chance factors
all play a part in a person's health status and life
chances. Drawing together his life experiences in
the context of food and health, Francois has some
simple advice to give:

"You can't tell people what to do. You can just
make them aware. Of course, governments can
regulate but thinking people worry about whether
they are all complicit with multinational companies in the global economy to put health at risk by
failing to take a proper grip. Those people who
grow their own food on allotments or in gardens understand the value of exercise, fresh air
and fresh organic food. They also know that their
apples or potatoes may not be glamorous – but
they are not toxic and taste good! I have come
a long way in my life from a small village in
France to the suburbs of a large city in England.
I love the people here and their culture. It would
be nice to see a greater emphasis at every level
on the value of healthy ingredients and the joy of
properly-cooked food at home and in restaurants.
In my early working years, business clients would

have lunches in a restaurant. These days, it is more likely that they will have a sandwich instead. There is more caution when it comes to desserts and sugar consumption. The challenge is to create tasty food, that does not contribute to poor health."

Perhaps the game-changer may be adjustments in the work/life balance. Some research has suggested that productivity is not affected by a reduction in the working week. If this were to be translated into a shorter working day, maybe there would be more time for home-grown ingredients and a resurgence of interest in healthy cooking. In such circumstances, would there be a place for restaurants and pubs offering family meals?

"The restaurant trade has been my life. Eating-out is not just about the food and wine. It is a social thing as well. As people get more leisure time, they will want to enjoy eating out with family and friends. What is on offer will depend on demand, so in the end people have the final say. That will never change - whatever the circumstances."

When analysing the contribution Francois has made to cooking and the restaurant trade, it can be said that he did not elect to emulate the master chefs who were his contemporaries by chasing the Michelin stars and the national and international accolades. Whilst he adhered to the culinary standards and the principles, he opted to cook for regular people who wanted to eat good food but could not always pay the fine-dining prices. That is not to say that he did not cook exceptional food or serve it to the discerning. He just preferred to concentrate largely front of house, understand his clients and ensure that they were served the tastes they relished, in surroundings they enjoyed and at prices they understood were good value. He was the ultimate showman, enthusiastic raconteur, keen musician and highly competent chef. His restaurants were always the destination for his followers - wherever he set up shop.

Whilst he has reached and worked well beyond the statutory retirement age, it will perhaps never be completely clear whether Francois has actually, finally and completely called it a day! He did, of course go beyond the time when most would have retired to the garden and put their feet up. Certainly, the amuse bouche starter, main course and dessert of his journey through the world of work has been gobbled-up enthusiastically. Only time will tell if there will be a 'cheese board,' but one thing is clear. His character, his personality, his banter and his food will forever be in the minds and the memory of all who had the pleasure of working with him or dining in his restaurants.

ACKNOWLEDGEMENT

I would like to thank Francois and Sue Primpied for their kind cooperation during the writing of this book. My gratitude is also extended to colleagues and business associates who worked with Francois over the years - including Jacques Meilhan, Mark Ciuffattelli, Derek Baugh Mike Clayphan and Callum Williams. I would also like to thank Christine Steele for her insights. Background information and images were obtained with permission from the hardback volume 'Bourg de Thizy' by Robert Mauger and Robert Dubuis.

John Maffin

All proceeds from the sale of this book are donated to Macmillan Cancer Support

BOOKS BY THIS AUTHOR

Waggy - The Ken Wagstaff Story

Years after his retirement, Ken Wagstaff remains a legend - particularly amongst fans at former clubs Mansfield Town and Hull City. A prolific goal-scorer, he terrorised English defences for fifteen years, amassing 303 career goals in 625 appearances. At various times he was tipped for international honours and his services coveted by top managers. The names of Waggy and his Booth-ferry Park strike partner Chris (Chillo) Chilton are indelibly written in the Tigers Hall of Fame.

ABOUT THE AUTHOR

John Maffin

John Maffin was born in Swanland, East Yorkshire. After several
years in retail management, he
joined a family retail and manu-
facturing business as a director.
In middle-age, he gained a first
class honours degree in Social Policy & Adminis-
tration at the University of Hull. Following post-
graduate study, he went on to complete 27 years
in NHS general practice management. During 18
years service in the police special constabulary, he
rose to the rank of Divisional Commandant. He
has also worked part-time as a university lecturer,
photojournalist and photographer. In addition to
being a published author, he is currently MD of a
technology company producing GP practice web-
sites and supplying AI solutions for the NHS and
other government agencies.

Printed in Great Britain
by Amazon

37413714R00116